D1615269

A Priest's Psychic Diary

A Priest's Psychic Diary

J. DOVER WELLMAN

Foreword by Richard Baker, O.B.E.

Ernest and Nina Keeling
with my prayers
J. Dover Wellman
30 Sept.. 1978 .

LONDON

SPCK

First published 1977
SPCK
Holy Trinity Church
Marylebone Road
London NW1 4DU

Printed in Great Britain by
Hollen Street Press Ltd., Slough

ISBN 0 281 03561 X

To
Dorothy, my wife,
who has so often shared my
psychic experiences

CONTENTS

FOREWORD

Every Christmas my family and I look forward to the annual Carol Service at Emmanuel Church, Hampstead; indeed, we would hate to miss it. Fortunately the Vicar (and the author of this book), Jack Dover Wellman, has been in the habit of asking me to contribute readings to the service for a number of years — so I always try to make sure someone else reads the News that night.

The special magic of the Emmanuel Carol Service stems partly from the West Indian music, steel band and all, which has been a traditional feature of the occasion since the days of that fine singer, Edric Connor; partly from the fact that, until prices finally made it impossible, the service was lit by hundreds of candles; but the quality of the evening, which always ends with a party in the vicarage, is created above all by the Vicar and his wife. There is an open welcome for all, and a sense that we are part of that infinitely larger family, seen and unseen, which is always drawn closer at Christmas.

Jack has spoken to me only occasionally about his psychic experiences — he once took part in a discussion on our Radio 4 programme *Start the Week* about exorcism — and I must admit my reaction bordered on the sceptical. However, I have always been deeply impressed by his sincerity and was very glad when the chance came, through this book, to learn more about the author's encounters with the world of the spirit and his methods of dealing with it. There are aspects of human nature which simply cannot be explained away, and the explanation offered here is deeply interesting. I also believe that Jack Dover Wellman's direct approach to spiritual healing (though he in no way claims to supplant the professional psychiatrist) will bring comfort and hope to many.

I am sure *A Priest's Psychic Diary* — controversial as it is — will be widely read and discussed. If we are honest, I'm sure most of us can recall more than one strange experience which might prompt us to say, with Hamlet:

> There are more things in heaven and earth, Horatio,
> Than are dreamt of in your philosophy.

RICHARD BAKER

PREFACE

Faith is the prerequisite and necessary stimulus of prayer. And it is prayer which can liberate most satisfactorily the extra-sensory perceptions. These, in turn, attest the reality and relevance of the spiritual realm. They intimate the presence of angels who desire to help us and of demons who may seek to harm us. They inform us through telepathy, clairvoyance, guidance, and prophecy. They heal us through peculiar powers and exorcism.

There is an increasing interest today in the study of extra-sensory perception. But such investigation is concerned with what material advantage may accrue from it rather than with how it could assist and advance religious belief. This concern, of course, comes more properly within the province of the Church, which unfortunately generally looks askance on psychic phenomena. She may regard them with complete suspicion or as unworthy of serious consideration, even at times dismissing them wholly as 'the works of the Devil'. However, the Church, being concerned with the *whole* personality of man, must regard *all* that pertains to his spiritual nature and then seek to transform it (by invoking faith in Jesus Christ) into a source of blessing.

There is nothing which can separate us from the love of God, and some psychic phenomena will actually serve to support and illuminate that truth most vividly. Without the supernatural element, of course, there can be no religion, and so the Church does a great disservice if she does not seek to understand more thoroughly the paranormal and, where appropriate, to foster it sensibly. She could thereby arouse the slumbering religious instinct of the present time and reveal how highly relevant is the spiritual realm to the life of man.

But faith, which is the prerequisite and the continuing stimulus of prayer, is intensely difficult to develop in an age which underlines so heavily the claims and desires of materialism. Here the Church may be weakening herself by undue concentration on social and political issues. These only serve to emphasize the pressures of the material world, whereas her priority should be in leading and instructing man in those things which inspire and enlighten his inmost soul and so certify to him the prime importance of the spiritual world. Then will he deal more ably with his problems in society.

St John's Gospel says that Thomas was not present when the risen Christ appeared to the other disciples in the Upper Room after the crucifixion. When he heard their story he declared that he could not believe the resurrection unless he too received the evidence of it even as his brethren had done. In consequence he has been rather unkindly dubbed 'Doubting' Thomas and maligned as the prime example of one who lacked faith. But to have honest doubt is no sin, and it is to be noted that although the risen Christ especially commended those who believe without the proof of sight, nevertheless he granted to Thomas the evidence he desired by appearing to him also eight days later, in his resurrection body. Only *after* that manifestation did he bid the disciple not to be faithless but henceforth to believe.

Today many, including some Christians, are like Thomas, inasmuch as they need some kind of psychic experience which will witness to them of the reality of the spiritual world. I have therefore written the first part of this book with the purpose of heartening those who need a little 'sight' to support their Christian beliefs. If its record of some of my own psychic experiences helps others in the continuing struggle of maintaining a lively and steady faith in this difficult (because highly materialistic) age, the tribute must go to the many men and women (and children too) who, often unaware of it, have given me glimpses of 'other-worldly' glory which I must treasure all my days.

Through what has happened in their lives, which I have been wonderfully privileged to share as their parson, has come an illumination of the spiritual world which has convinced me again and again of the truth which is in Jesus Christ, and of the nearness to us of that spiritual realm which the Church colourfully describes as being the dwelling of 'angels and archangels and all the company of Heaven'.

I felt, however, I could not leave the matter without some reflection upon the mysterious working of the soul and of the valuable assistance which, I believe, extra-sensory perceptions can afford to religion. Hence the second part of this book, for which I acknowledge my debt to Abbot Weisinger's *Occult Phenomena in the Light of Theology*,* particularly for his exposition on the 'body-soul, spirit-soul' concept.

I must add my thanks to Mrs Eve Walber for making a careful edited choice among the many incidents I recorded in my original manuscript. Without her help, the book would have been overlong.

J. DOVER WELLMAN

Emmanuel Vicarage
Hampstead, London
1977

*Published by Cardinal Books, 1957.

INTRODUCTION

Is it pure fancy to believe that in the moment of birth spiritual powers are released to protect us and help our future course? I do not think so. Indeed I believe that angelic powers have often guarded me in times of perplexity and crisis, and have protected me in moments of danger.

During the First World War, in April 1917, *HMS Swift*, a vessel of the Dover Patrol, together with *HMS Broke* engaged the enemy in the Channel. It was a successful encounter, as the country came to know when Commander Evans of the *Broke* made his triumphal return to Dover. Either during this battle or in one of the many patrols the hull of the *Swift* scraped the chains of a mine which, however, failed to explode. My father was in the engine-room when this occurred. With bated breath he had heard the ominous scraping noise, and his terrified suspense had been followed by intense relief as this awesome sound died away.

The next morning the commander of the *Swift* sent for him. 'News has been received', he told him, 'that a son has been born to you. Promise me something. When you name him will you call him "Jack" after the sea and "Dover" in memory of our Patrol? Do this because he brought us great luck last night.' And so it was to be. They say that those who sail the seas sometimes have more than an ordinary measure of superstition. What is probably nearer the truth is to say that their calling keeps them in surer touch with spiritual realities.

Seventeen years later I began my working life as an apprentice in H.M. Dockyard, Portsmouth. One Saturday morning, in the early days of my training, I was passing a

1

caisson where a ship was undergoing a major re-fit, and I was suddenly attracted by excited shouting and hectic activity. Looking over the side of the dock I could see below me the foredeck, on which a heavy gun was mounted. This enormous weapon was being slung in a giant crane. Two men who had been working underneath the gun had been trapped as the slinging had slipped. The safety precaution of shoring up the massive weight had either not been taken or that, too, had capsized.

The ghastly result was that one man was crushed completely flat and the other was pinned down by the lower half of his body. Gradually this man was freed and his inert form hauled up to the dockside to the ambulance, but the mangled shape of his companion lay spreadeagled in blood upon the deck. It was the first time I had witnessed violent death, and this particular tragedy was so gruesome that the horror of it clung about me all through the day. The shock of it left me so numb and shaken that I walked around as if in some continuing nightmare.

That same evening I had arranged to go to a church social. Most of my childhood and early youth had been spent in the all-absorbing life of one of the best-known parish churches in England, St Mark's, Portsea, and the social was being run by a daughter church. As the evening passed I became more and more restless and suddenly could stand the atmosphere of merriment no longer. As I walked out of the parish hall I knew I must go into the church just opposite. A force outside myself seemed to compel me.

I stood looking towards the altar. The turmoil in my mind cried out to be understood and relieved. The great question tormenting me was how to reconcile that morning's scene of tragic horror with the brightness of the love of God in which I so ardently believed. For the first time in my life I was facing what we all have to face: the question of how our faith can stand up against the imperfections and misfortunes of this world.

Then it happened: a vision which was the first consciously remembered one of my life. The altar began to glow with a white radiance, and every detail of it became clear as if a searchlight were playing upon it. Then a strange compulsion made me concentrate my eyes on the cross above it. As I looked the radiance around the altar began to settle on that cross, which otherwise was hardly discernible in the darkness, and slowly I began to see a form take shape upon it.

I prayed without ceasing — prayers I cannot remember save only that I wanted so desperately to know what I must do. As I prayed in that deep anguish of spirit, with all the pent-up emotions of that strange day passing over me in engulfing waves, I saw at last quite clearly that figure on the cross. It was shining with a wonderful glory.

I knew I was seeing the Lord Jesus Himself. So beautiful and joyful was this vision that I felt I must be in another world, that my soul must have left my body. It gave me an ineffable feeling, an exhilarating infusion of incredible power and certainty which filled my whole being. And then a voice spoke, gently but commandingly. It told me that I must give my life to the ministry of the Church.

The wonder of that experience transformed my world. The shock of the morning now held no more terror. It was not that any philosophy had evolved about the misfortunes of human life. There were no logical answers revealed, no clearing up of the puzzle into a neat and tidy explanation. The revelation went far beyond that. It gave not solutions but, what was far more inspiring, an inward peace, a total confidence in the all-prevailing and conquering love of God. Above all it pointed the way for my future life.

I knew I must work for some years and save from my wages until the expense of theological training could be met. In those days there were no financial grants to assist candidates. Five years later, by 1939, I had achieved my goal and saved enough money. I was due to go up to Oxford at Michaelmas that year. But the outbreak of the

Second World War gave me no other choice than to continue my experiments and research work for the Admiralty, which were considered of national importance until the end of hostilities.

So six more years of waiting before my theological training could begin. Then, at long last, at the age of thirty came the crowning joy of receiving the laying-on of hands in ordination. It was the wonderful experience of that vision thirteen long years before which had held me firm to the call it had given me.

Part 1
Encounters

A TRANSFIGURATION

On Sunday morning, 5 October 1947, I was ordained a deacon in Rochester Cathedral. The next day my vicar gave me a short list of sick persons to visit. That list grew steadily longer as my contacts in the parish widened. But I remain especially and eternally grateful for those first few names, since it included one who was to awaken me dramatically to the healing aspect of my future ministry.

Rose lived in a small bungalow in a quiet little side street. Her husband, George, was a retired railway worker, a gentle and courteous man. Both were devout church people and had been regular worshippers together until the disease which afflicted Rose had become so deep-seated that she could no longer be taken to church even in an invalid chair. When I came to know her she was in an advanced stage of osteo-arthritis, and so terribly ravaged by it that her limbs were cruelly distorted into the most painful and odd shapes. Her fingers and toes, arms and legs were turned against the joints.

In those early visits I would just sit with the couple and make general conversation. She would be more or less reclining in her bed and he would be seated near the foot of it on an old wicker chair, while I was always pressed to occupy the 'best chair'. He would sit puffing at his pipe while she would tell me about the old days, about the church which meant so much to both of them, and of their former activities for it. Out would come the best china for tea, often with some cake George had made.

Many a quiet and pleasant afternoon we spent together, though gradually there was growing in my mind the pressing thought that 1 must try to do more than just chat with them. But shyness seemed to inhibit me from talking about spiritual things. Perhaps I felt that such patent examples of Christian love in such a truly Christian marriage did not need pious conversation from me and that it would be humbug to presume they did. Nevertheless the nagging concern that I was failing them badly in a spiritual sense continued to bother me deeply.

Then a day came which was to change my whole attitude and to bring special enlightenment to my ministry. As I knocked on their front door I could hear a sound like someone crying. George eventually appeared in the doorway. His face was ashen. In a very disturbed voice he said simply: 'Rose is in such pain. She wants to go home.' This, I knew, was his way of saying she wanted to die. Up till then I had never heard her speak of her pain though it must have been intense and almost always with her.

At the far end of the little passage I could hear her sobbing. It was a heart-rending sound and sent a chill of horror and distress right through me. As I followed George towards that familiar room where his wife was lying I experienced the most unutterable sense of helplessness and frustration. The agitation in me which had been growing slowly but relentlessly during the past weeks seemed now to have come to a head. What earthly good was my ministry? What use was it when, faced as I was now with the spectacle of such anguish, I could do nothing to alleviate it? What answer was there to all this? Certainly no lectures in pastoralia and psychology at theological college had equipped me to face a situation like this.

Over and over, as I walked those few steps to her room, that biting question: 'What can I do?' was joined to the deepest plea: 'O God, help me. Help me to help her.' First this turmoil of feeling, of hopelessness and helplessness. Then, finally, the casting of all into the hands of God, as a last resort — an act of complete abandon. The astounding thing was that this 'casting of my burden upon the Lord' resulted in a sudden surge into me of confidence

7

and power. I did not know precisely what I must do. Not just then, that is. But the sense of utter relief was amazing and immediately uplifting.

As I entered the room I hardly took in the moaning form upon the bed, torturedly twisting and jerking in the excruciating pain. What would have daunted me previously in such a sight did not do so now. For I *knew* what I must do though I did not then know *why* I must do it. Calmly and purposefully I approached the bedside and without any further preliminary simply knelt by it, at the same time gently taking one of those twisting and clutching hands in mine.

All the while it was if someone other than myself were taking charge of all my action, and my thoughts as well.

And I prayed. I had no thought of what to pray or why I chose the prayer I did. I would have said it was chosen for me. It seemed to come bubbling up from the very depths of my being, but nevertheless deliberately, meaningfully, exultantly: 'Our Father, which art in heaven, hallowed be thy name. . .'. The Lord's own prayer. Now I had closed my eyes. The sombre little room was shut from view. I felt as if I were alone with this poor anguished creature. Alone, but not alone, for I could see the figure of Christ. He was kneeling in prayer to the Father, as he may have looked in the Garden of Gethsemane.

It was when I reached the words, 'thy kingdom come on earth as it is in heaven' that the full vision came and I observed a pure transformation. For I was forced, or so it seemed, to open my eyes. The room was filled with a dazzling white light. Her hand in mine was now lying still. Between it and my own there was a strange, warm, steady throbbing, as if the electric currents of our lives were mingling in one great coursing flow.

I looked at her and saw the face of a young girl, beautiful to behold. Every deep line of age and of the years of pain was erased. Her face was quite radiant, glowing with

8

some peculiar brilliance which appeared to be coming from within the flesh and rising to the surface to transform it. And she was murmuring: 'Oh, how wonderful, how wonderful. All the pain is gone.' Fascinated, caught up in the sheer beauty and wonder of what I was looking at, aware of this great pulsing of power through my whole body, I went on with the prayer. I knew that I was witnessing the reality of the spiritual world, a true vision. Language beggars the glorious loveliness and tremendous sense of power of this transcendent experience. It was a glorious transport.

This was something which I felt was more real than anything this world offers. It was certainly no trick of lighting, for outdoors the day was overcast with the threat of thunder, but this brilliant light was persisting, and the strange power was throbbing on and on between us. The woman was lying so relaxed, *and her face transfigured*. These things I saw. And instinctively I knew that she was also experiencing something akin to all that I was now perceiving. To this amazing sight there was now added yet another dimension. For as I came to the ending of the prayer of Jesus: 'for thine is the kingdom, the power and the glory', I could hear a strange sound. Somehow or other, though I do not know why, I connected this with the beating of angels' wings. By this I do not mean that I think angels possess wings in the literal sense. But the sound was like that of moving wings, or the rustle of the wind. At any rate, this notion of angels' wings occurred to me as I heard it.

All I can say for certain is that I understood how the disciples needed the symbolic language they used when trying to describe the coming of the gift of the Holy Spirit to them, the empowering Spirit of Jesus, on the Day of Pentecost. They declared they saw light about their heads like tongues of fire and heard a sound like a rushing wind. There was light, strange and beautiful, about this woman's head and face, and there was a sound which betokened great power and yet the caress of love. Beyond that I cannot explain. All words fail. Several moments passed before that experience faded. I felt that this was something beyond time, of the nature of eternity — an incomparable bliss.

I left Rose marvellously content. The ineffable sweetness of her look was something I treasure to this day. Always afterwards, though her arthritis troubled her still, she would eagerly wait for that moment when, at the end of my visits, I would take her hand in mine and say a prayer for the healing touch of Jesus Christ. The blazing beauty of that first experience was not to be so vividly repeated, but always there was the sense of healing power flowing through me and into her as we prayed together. Then, always, the ensuing calm and peace. Never again did she suffer so severe a bout of pain.

I left her that day with the knowledge of a new dimension having been given to my ministry. It was born of the recognition that out of our own resources alone we can do nothing, but when we give ourselves over in all our inadequacy to the Father, he makes us strong to work his will. It is he, his life, his love, his healing, who works in and through us, and to receive these gifts we must abandon ourselves completely to him without a trace of self-sufficiency.

I knew then that among the purposes of my ministry must be this one of healing. There are other gifts of the Spirit, no one gift superior to another. But it is this particular one which I believe the Father has committed to me, the laying-on of hands with prayer. That day I knew also the complementary result of such experiences. That is, we are not left upon the beautiful mount of transfiguration but must come down from it to meet again the sorrows, testings and disappointments of the imperfect world below. The spiritual experience is not given to us to bask in, withdrawing from the life around us, but in order that we may be active reflections of it to those who sit in any kind of darkness.

We have also to realize that where there are people who have no faith or in whom suffering has made faith grow dim, we ourselves must become faith for them. Jesus taught that truth when he observed the faith of the four men who lowered the litter bearing their paralysed young friend through the roof of Peter's house. It is recorded that 'seeing *their* faith' our Lord was able to heal the youth.

The great agony of her physical pain had robbed Rose temporarily of the tranquillity and certainty of her faith. In her hour of need it was laid upon me, in my own health and freedom from physical suffering, to exercise complete faith for her.

A HEALING LETTER

I believe that in every instance of the laying-on of hands with prayer there is healing. I cannot record all the occasions in which I have exercised this particular sphere of my ministry because they are too numerous. But I do not wish on the other hand to give the impression that only the more dramatic cases are what matter. Where the prayer of compassion is made and where the issue is laid unreservedly in the hands of God, healing always follows. Whether that healing is recognized or not is another matter.

Healing is never withheld. We may not observe it each time in the re-constitution of the physical body but always in the invigoration of the spirit. Nor is healing provided according to our merits or deserts. The newness of life God gives us, like his love, mercy, and forgiveness, is given freely. The only possible withholding of his healing would be where there was no personal desire for it.

Quite early in my ministry I was asked to see a young widow with tuberculosis. Probably as the aftermath of the strains and shortages of war there was a great deal of this disease during the latter part of the forties and early fifties. Her husband had died a few months earlier from the same illness. She had two young children, one of whom was not yet old enough for school so that for most of the day it was impossible for her to get the rest she needed, and continually difficult to prevent the children from spending too much time around her bed.

Her elderly mother was now the only help in the house, and she was very deaf and partially blind. The young mother was in an agonizing situation, and it was evident that the long strain of nursing her husband had ended at last in her catching his disease. By the time I was asked to call she had almost reached breaking point though she tried to maintain a brave face in front of her mother and her children and, I gathered, before the doctor, too.

I was deeply moved by her story. 'I don't believe there's any hope for me. What will happen to the children?' As she finished telling me, with tears in her eyes, I had a kind of sixth sense that she would certainly recover. I looked at her for a moment and then said: 'I don't believe that because your husband died of this that you will. I am quite sure in fact that you are going to get well and, what is more, very much quicker than you now think possible.' In saying this I did not feel I was taking a shot in the dark or just trying to cheer her up. Something inside me was driving me to speak in this way and assuring me also of the truth of my words. Clearly some sense of this strange confidence in me communicated itself to her, for she brightened visibly.

I then spoke about the healing power of prayer, after which I said: 'I am going to lay my hands upon you and God will give you his healing as we pray.' Placing my hands on her head I prayed quite simply: 'Lord Jesus, present with us now, lay thy hands of healing on this thy child.' Then, after a short pause of quiet during which I felt a tingling warmth and vibration in my hands, I said: 'We thank you, Lord, for Thy healing. Amen.' I left her with her eyes still closed, telling her to remain for a while as quiet as possible.

When I returned home I felt powerfully impelled to write a letter to the medical authorities. I urged that this woman be considered a priority for a hospital bed and treatment. I did this despite the fact that she had been told there was almost no chance of her going away for such care because the waiting list was long and her home circumstances not as bad as some.

The reply was somewhat stereotyped and disappointing. I was assured her case was always under consideration, but

13

there was a great shortage of beds. My delight, therefore, was exceeded only by that of the young widow when she told me on my next visit, scarcely a week later, that she had been informed she would be taken into hospital within a few days. And so she was, to a newly opened hospital which she described in a letter to me as 'simply wonderful'. But the real joy was yet to be. For after what proved to be a remarkably short time in that hospital she came home completely cured.

Of course one can take the simple, straightforward view that her healing came wholly through the normal treatment of medical science in that hospital. Yet the fact remains that a woman who was almost at the end of her tether had her confidence suddenly restored by the laying-on of hands. Also, the strange foreknowledge of her unexpectedly speedy cure which I had received during that ministration proved accurate.

The fact is that prayer, in some mysterious fashion, sets in motion forces which bring relief, strengthening, and peace of mind. More things are indeed wrought by prayer than this world dreams of. All the power for the life of mankind to be whole, that is healthy, is present in this universe which the God of infinite love has made for us temporarily to dwell in. And prayer is the key to it. Yet we do not know how prayer connects us with this power. All we know is that prayer acts as a link which is needed to contact that power and become a medium of it. That power is equally mysterious in its manner of working and does not always produce obvious results.

Though I listened intently to this young widow's sad story when I first met her, that did not prevent me from holding open one part of my mind to make a silent offering of her tragedy to God. This is my usual practice when I listen to people's troubles; while I listen I pray. As the tale is told I am asking God to give his healing, his help, his guidance and asking, too, that he make me a channel of his wisdom. So silent prayer had already been offered before I

14

actually gave her the laying-on of hands with spoken prayer. I believe this 'prayer of seeking' opens up the intake of God's power and that this then provided me with that total sense of confidence.

That letter, I believe, conveyed the power canalized by the prayers I had offered. Even as I wrote, each word seemed to burn upon the paper with a radiance which convinced me that it would be the vehicle of a divine blessing. When I had finished it, I held it to my forehead for some moments to release into it the assurance that was now pouring from my deepest being. Thus, I believe, it became charged with the supreme power of God. Now it was a sacrament, a visible sign of that invisible certainty of God's caring. It was in that triumphal conviction that I posted it. And hospital doors were promptly opened.

A BURDENED CONSCIENCE

One Sunday evening I preached a sermon in which I mentioned divine healing. Afterwards a woman who was then attending the church for the first time asked me if I would call and see her husband. She told me his story.

He had been a grocer with a most successful business. One night, after closing the shop, he said he was going for a walk. Hours later he had not returned. His wife finally contacted the police who, much later, reported that he had been found in another part of London in a dark street with his wrists slashed. His condition when he was discovered was very serious, and for a long while his life hung in the balance. At last he was discharged from hospital and allowed to return home. But he came back a wreck. His suicide attempt had left him with a weakened heart. From a former life of great activity he was now reduced to being incapable of anything which required more than minimum effort.

At the earliest opportunity I called upon the couple. After a minute or two of polite conversation his wife strategically withdrew in order to leave me alone with him. Almost immediately after she had left the room he turned to me with great earnestness. 'She's told you about me', he began. 'I know she thinks I may try to do it again but I wouldn't. I only wish I could make her feel sure about that. It's an awful strain for her because I know she is agitated whenever she has to go out and leave me here.'

'She would be more likely to believe you', I replied, 'if you were not so morose, don't you think? She tells me that you are so often sunk in gloom that, quite naturally, she becomes very apprehensive about you.' 'But I wouldn't', he remonstrated. 'I swear I wouldn't try it again. How can I make her believe it?' Since the moment of meeting him I had been praying silently the prayer of seeking. I must discover in what way I could help.

Then, as I looked at his anxious face, a question arose in my mind. It came suddenly and without conscious deliberation on my part, as if someone other than myself were putting it. It proved the very tinder which kindled the fire of complete frankness.

'You still have something very deep burdening your mind, haven't you?' I asked. 'What is it?' As I spoke further inspiration seemed to come. I went on: 'I know that it isn't just this suicide attempt. It's something else — perhaps what drove you to make it. I know you confessed to feeling overcome with the stress of your work. That's what everyone thinks and believes is the full reason. But there is more to it than that, isn't there?'

The words came from me with simple directness. I I had been given a profound insight. Psychic forces were at work. I had the feeling that I was reading his soul. Then it came in a flash, a pure revelation. 'It concerned an association you had with another woman', I said. Though I gave this the inflection of a question I knew it was a statement of fact.

For a moment he looked at me in great surprise, almost dumbfounded. But this gave way to a sigh, as of relief. 'How you guessed that', he answered, 'is a mystery. But you are quite right. I was unfaithful. My wife didn't know and still doesn't. The affair is all over and I can't see that it can do any good to grieve her more with knowing it now. I was so ashamed at the time, and I am still. There were complications piling up all round me then because of it. I was in sheer mental agony. I could not see a way through. But, you see, it doesn't hurt me now. At least not as it did. I suppose I view things in a new way. What does hurt and worry me is that I think my dear wife still fears me having another go at taking my life. Honestly I wouldn't, but I do

get these fearful depressions when I think about everything over and over again.'

As he poured it all out I felt as if I were following a
clear and searching light which was showing me precisely
what I must say and do next. It was like being under the
control of a superior intelligence which knew all the answers and the real heart of the problem in this man's tor-
mented spirit. The prayer of seeking had disclosed the way
of healing. So what followed I can only describe as being
the result of divine guidance.

'You say you are truly sorry for the past', I said. 'I believe you because you have said that things look different
now. That is the sign of repentance, a real change of heart,
a new attitude. So I am going to give you absolution. That
is one of my duties and powers as a priest. From then on
you will not, and must not, carry this burden of the past
with you. God has forgiven you. His will now is that you
start life anew in that wonderful knowledge.'

Then, placing my hands on his head, I pronounced his
forgiveness in the name of our heavenly Father. Several
tremors shook his body as I did so. His shoulders heaved in
great sobs of emotion. Then there fell on us both so deep a
sense of calm and quiet that it appeared almost tangible.
It was as if the air had become still and we were suspended
in tranquillity. Words defy these ecstatic sensations, but I
am sure this experience was shared by the man also.

Finally I removed my hands and said: 'Remember, then,
now and always that this sin of the past is done with. Do
not allow it to haunt you or to discolour your life from
now on. God has forgiven you. Now you must recreate
harmony between your wife and yourself. And in this endeavour, you know, God's Spirit will be helping you.'

His eyes were closed and there was an expression of
great relief on his face. The feeling of something transcendent still seemed to hang in the atmosphere of the
room. My next action again appeared to be taken under
some special sort of compulsion, as though I were being

18

urged to be an instrument of the power that filled the very air about us. I said: 'God is asking me now to give you his healing for your body.' I placed my hands over his chest and prayed: 'In the Name of Jesus Christ who loves you, receive now his healing.'

He was still quiet. My action did not seem to surprise him. In fact when I looked back later, it seemed to me that the whole interview was like a series of events which had a spontaneous thread of continuity running through them. There was nothing forced, nothing jarring. Psychic guidance was running true and clear. We were in the sure and certain hands of God's benevolence. So it was that the man appeared to be expecting what I did, and even eagerly awaiting it.

I did not remove my hands for what must have been at least a full minute. Immediately the prayer for healing had been spoken there was a tingling like pins and needles in my hands and a sense of great warmth. After a moment or two I became very conscious of the erratic beating of his heart. Then his pulse began to gear itself to a gentle and certain motion which appeared gradually to accord with that of my own.

It was like holding a frightened bird. First the uncertain fluttering and then, as calm and confidence is established, the peaceful relaxation, the end of all fear and tension. It was a remarkable sensation and yet completely easy and natural. When the feeling of a definite flow of power through me had ended I said: 'We thank you so much, dear Lord, for this your healing.' As I left him, still sitting quiet and relaxed, I said: 'You know you have received great healing today. Don't worry any more. The Lord is with you.' In the hall I said good-bye to his wife. 'He will be all right', I assured her. 'I know it.'

She met me only a few days later in the street and said excitedly: 'I was just coming to tell you. It's absolutely wonderful. He's up and about for the first time. The morning after you came to us he walked down to the library.

19

Now he's talking about redecorating the kitchen for me. I never expected such a quick change. But best of all he is so much happier in himself: things are so much better between us. It is as if we have started life all over again closer to each other than ever before. The doctor is quite amazed and most pleased with him. I'm so thankful I asked you to come. And you know I might not have done so if you had not said the things you did on that Sunday night in the service.'

4

A VISION OF HEALING

The prayer for healing cannot be assessed on quick or obvious results, yet now and then it does produce an immediate, remarkable change. I was asked one day to visit a woman who was gravely ill. She lived with her very aged parents, one of whom was extremely deaf and the other almost blind. The house was gloomy and depressing, and the mother, nearly ninety, was so deaf and near-sighted that I had difficulty in explaining who I was and the purpose of my visit when she answered the door to me.

She led me to a bedroom upstairs, where I saw an amazing sight. Had it not been so sad and serious an errand I think I would have been amused by a scene which could have come straight from a novel by Dickens. On a large, ornate bed in the spacious, sombre room lay the woman whom I had come to see. She was so enveloped by the great heap of pillows which propped her up that I could scarcely see her face. Round the bed sat five elderly females drinking tea and totally absorbed in conversation with each other. None appeared to take the slightest notice of the invalid herself nor to be aware of my own presence.

After waiting patiently for a while I finally forced their attention by taking one of them by the elbow and introducing myself. At last their chattering ceased and they stared at me curiously. Then, almost with one voice, they proceeded to inform me how very ill the sick woman was. To my amazement she struggled up from the mound of pillows and pronounced that all this was very true and that she did not expect to live much longer. With a forced, cheerful indifference and rather too loud a laugh, she said: 'I'm not bothered. The doctors can't do any more with

21

this illness. I'll probably be dead within a month or two. But I don't mind.'

Her tone was almost flippant and rather daunted me at first. The general air of somewhat callous acceptance of her fate was most disconcerting. The scene began to resemble a Shakespearean tragedy, the group round her bed like harpies rejoicing in an approaching death. I managed, however, to manoeuvre myself between the five ladies, and standing beside the bed said loudly to the sick woman: 'I would like to see you for a few moments alone, if I may.'

My words had the desired effect. After a great deal of clatter in the piling of cups and saucers we were finally left alone. I have often found that when I have been most anxious and eager to help I have had an initial set-back. Perhaps the reason is that one may thus be given an opportunity to reassess the situation and compelled to rely more fully upon God. One's own self must always take a back seat so that absolute dependence upon him may be consciously acknowledged.

The moment her companions had gone a sure sense of what must be done came to me. I held her hand and, looking directly into her eyes, said: 'You are not going to die. I am quite sure about that. But I sense that you are terribly sad about something. Perhaps even bitter. Will you tell me what it is?' My words and the question appeared to come from some mysterious source beyond myself.

Now quite suddenly her mask of bravado fell away and she began to cry piteously. Through the tears she poured out to me all her inner pain and resentment. In essence this was that she had given up her youth, her very life, for the sake of her parents. She had been born to them very late in their lives. Now her father was totally blind and her mother so deaf that for long it had been impossible to have any real communication with either. The old couple had depended upon her care and nursing for many years.

There had been the chance once, she said, of marriage, but she had foregone it because she believed it to be her

duty to remain at her parents' side in their increasing in-
capacity. In the first years of her illness she had managed to
carry on almost normally but now it had become necessary
for her to take to her bed for ever-increasing periods, so
that the household was practically dependent on the help
given in turn by those five women I had seen with her.

Clutching nervously at my hand with both of hers, she
said she felt the agony of what she considered had been a
wasted life. There was added anguish in that the parents
for whom she had sacrificed so much were now so senile
that they could not take in her present plight nor appreciate
at all what she had done for them. Then her voice trembled
so much I could not distinguish further words. There was
another awful burst of sobbing. It was terrible to see and
hear.

This flood of feeling, obviously long pent up in her, continued for several minutes with shattering intensity. The
anguish of it seemed to pour into my own being. I felt
utterly powerless to give her any comfort and, in the distress of that realization, I cried out within myself for God
to help her. Suddenly it was as if my soul had taken wings.
I felt as if I were seeing into the future with amazing
clarity. And what I could see was this woman, brimming
with new health and buoyant with happiness. Her sick
body lying on the bed seemed to dissolve before my eyes
and then she appeared, radiantly cheerful and standing upright, in front of me.

This vision remained long enough and vivid enough to
give me complete confidence in her restoration to health
and happiness. Almost simultaneously she recovered suf-
ficient composure for me to speak to her again. I repeated
that I did not believe she was dying and pointed out that a
life given for the sake of others, even if they did not appear
to appreciate the sacrifice, was not a wasted life. It was a
life of the highest quality, as it had been in Jesus Christ.

Risking her thinking me eccentric, or melodramatic, I
told her of the vision I had just had of her complete

recovery. 'You really believe I shall get well?' she asked, and her eyes were eager with hope. 'You really saw me well and strong?'

'Indeed', I answered, and continued: 'In the laying-on of hands with prayer great help is given by God. You have told me much. Now tell me what gives you most anxiety about your present condition.' For answer she suddenly swung one leg out of bed. It was swathed with a bandage which she proceeded to unwind until I stopped her and asked: 'What is the trouble?' 'I have the most awful ulcers', she explained. 'They have not healed for ages. They are awful — just awful.'

'We shall pray,' I said, 'and I will place my hands above them. Let us be quiet for a few moments so that we can recollect together that we are in the loving and healing presence of God.' So we entered into the quietness for a while. The extraordinary vision I had had lingered in my mind, maintaining my confidence and faith and inspiring my next actions.

I noticed that she had closed her eyes. I had taken one of her hands in mine as we sought the strength and relaxation of stillness. Soon it seemed to me that the very air around us was buoyant with assurance and a great tenderness. In that moment I gathered an exhilarating impression that this sad woman and myself were receiving an inflow of rich, new life from him who is the Life.

I felt impelled to speak aloud. There was no hesitancy, no fumbling for what to say, only a blazing conviction that we had been given a blessed assurance. 'In thy name, Lord Jesus, heal this child of thine.' Even while speaking I felt the words were not all mine. Some other spirit was forming them for me and filling them with power.

There was no need for my hands to touch the bandaged limb, for when they were several inches above it there was tingling warmth in my fingertips. My palms burned and prickled as if invisible threads of power were linking us. When this sensation had passed I looked at her again. She

24

was very quiet and her eyes were closed. She was very composed and there was no trace of her former resentful expression.

'You will find the ulcers will soon heal now', I said. I had the sudden thought that this was too audacious a statement to make but dismissed it promptly as unworthy in the light of that extraordinary vision and of the certainty of healing during those few seconds of the laying-on of hands.

As I was leaving she said: 'Why did you say I was not dying?' 'It is as I have said', I answered. 'I had a clear vision of you fully recovered. I can't explain these things. It is a feeling deep inside which makes one certain. I am convinced that God reveals these things to us sometimes. You now believe you will get better, don't you?' The pallor had left her cheeks and there was a clear brightness in her eyes. 'Yes, I do believe it. I believe what you have said. I want to thank God for this wonderful day. Will you help me to do that?' So together we made a prayer of thanksgiving to God for his healing in that hour.

I went to see her again a few days later. To my amazement she herself answered the door. She was fully dressed and her manner jubilant. Excitedly she said: 'The ulcers have dried up. The first time for years. It's wonderful — a miracle. The doctor was astounded when I said what had happened.'

I was shortly to move to another parish, and as a thanksgiving she did some embroidery to give to my wife as a farewell present. She finished it in three days and brought it to our house. The change in her general appearance was quite remarkable. I could scarcely believe her to be the same person whom I had seen so wan and unhappy hardly a week earlier. She was radiantly cheerful and so full of gratitude.

Most likely her illness was primarily psychosomatic. When offered sympathetic understanding of the burden she endured and assured of complete recovery the

25

mysterious power of God's Holy Spirit had brought physical healing. Her real need had been for faith in the divine love and pity to be stimulated in her.

5

AN ENCOURAGING VOICE

I met great discouragement again in the case of a family who had been involved in a road accident. The father was driving a motor cycle, carrying his teenage daughter pillion and his wife in the side-car. They had a bad collision with a lorry and all three were taken to the same hospital. I went to see them all in turn. The father and his daughter were comparatively fortunate; their injuries were not serious, but the wife's condition was highly critical. Having first seen the father and daughter, who begged me to find out how she was, I went to the ward where the wife had been taken.

I spoke to the sister in charge and asked if I might see the woman. Although on very rare occasions nurses can be a little off-hand, this was the only time in thirty years of innumerable visits to hospitals that I met anything like real hardness. The clergy are usually allowed to visit hospital patients at times other than the normal visiting hours, provided, of course, it is practicable. The manner of this nurse, however, was obviously calculated to be as awkward as possible and to make me feel that my visit was quite unnecessary.

'Surely you know already', she said, 'she has been unconscious all the time ever since she was brought in. She won't know you or be aware of you in any way. We don't expect that she will recover consciousness.' For a moment I felt very disconcerted and disheartened, more by her manner than by what she had said. My first reaction was to think of retreating there and then and leaving the hospital. It did seem rather pointless to stand by the bed of an unconscious, dying person whom, in any case, I had never seen before.

'Besides, the screens are around her', the nurse went on, seeing that she had succeeded in making me hesitate. 'Oh, I would not want them moved, Sister', I said, not wanting to cause the slightest inconvenience. For answer she looked at me as if this were the end of the matter, and that now I would leave immediately, seeing how nonsensical my visit must be.

I was about to turn away when something made me hold my ground. Quite clearly, I heard a voice within me say: 'Go on. Go on and say your prayer. You must say it. This woman will recover.' The voice and the feeling it aroused in me were so positive and insistent that I found myself speaking as with a will that overrode my own, saying to the nurse: 'All the same, I would like to go over to her bed, and just stand for a moment outside the screens.' This time she just waved her hand. 'Oh, all right,' she said, 'but I've told you she will not know you are here. She's completely unconscious. She certainly won't hear you.'

Relieved, I walked to the far end of the ward. The other patients watched me curiously. Then I stood still for a few moments outside the screens. Through a small gap between them I could just glimpse the woman lying there with her head almost completely swathed in bandages. As I stood there I entered a trance condition. There was no conscious intention to do so, but it just happened and quite suddenly. Again the voice within insisted that I say my prayers. It was a very strange experience. I felt engulfed by some other presence and yet I had not lost my own identity. I felt that I was an instrument. Even that does not really describe the extraordinary sensation of those moments.

My prayer was of the simplest. Purely an arrow for God's help. But it was not a mere plea. It was more an assertion, as if I knew already that the power of God's healing had been given, even as the prayer was made. There was absolutely no doubt in me of her recovery from that moment. A strange but lovely aura of quiet and peace settled all around me. The rest of my thoughts were just a jumble of emotions, joy, thanksgiving, the sense of a wonderful added dimension to life. I had stayed only a few seconds outside those screens, but I felt every eye in that ward was now watching me with intense interest as I came away. There was the most peculiar stillness in the place, as if all were spellbound. My prayer had been a silent one, though some of those nearby may have seen my lips moving.

When I passed the nurse on my way out and said good-night, she stared back. Somewhat strangely, I thought, as if she too felt something of the spiritual power in the atmosphere or maybe perceived in me the sense of exaltation which I was feeling so strongly. Her eyes now had a sweetness I had not seen earlier, and for the first time she smiled. This all added to the glorious experience which impelled me back to see the father and daughter again in the other wards. I told each in turn that they must not worry unduly for I was certain they would be hearing some good news in a few hours.

The next morning my vicar greeted me with: 'You know that family who were in the accident? Well, the husband telephoned me from the hospital first thing this morning. He was most excited. Apparently his wife recovered consciousness during the night for the first time since the crash. They say there is such a marked change in her condition that she will recover. Have you been to the hospital yet to see them?' He did not know of my visit the evening before.

She did recover, and I have often asked myself about that strange foreknowledge I had received by the side of her unconscious body. Whose voice did I hear that urged me to go on and gave me the certainty that she would recover despite all the gloomy forecasts given me about her? Why did I feel engulfed by some dominating presence which nevertheless still allowed me to be acutely aware of my own personality? What brought on that condition of trance, for which there had been only the briefest, if any, mental or spiritual preparation, and which had followed so soon after that discouraging encounter with the nurse?

Was there some telepathic communication between myself and the unconscious woman or was there, on the other hand, the effective mediation of a guardian angel? In Christian terms all can be embraced under the heading of the working and influence of the Holy Spirit since in him all spiritual powers for good reside. All I can do is to record the case and give, very inadequately because language cannot encompass the transcendental, some inkling of the sensations and reactions involved. There are unique moments when, quite unexpectedly, we are poised, as it were, between two worlds, and for me, this was one of them.

6

IN TIME FOR THE WEDDING

Nervous ailments often respond most quickly to spiritual healing. I recall a young bride-to-be who for some months had been afflicted by a skin rash. This worried her more and more as the day of her wedding approached. All medical treatment was ineffective, and her doctor had told her that the trouble was caused by nervous tension.

Her parents and the young woman herself were keen church people, and about a fortnight before the marriage the girl's mother, knowing of my practice of spiritual healing, wrote to me asking if I would see her daughter to give her the laying-on of hands. So, just a week before the wedding, mother and daughter visited me in London.

The girl, a highly intelligent person, talked to me quite freely. Clearly she recognized that her difficulty lay in her very sensitive and emotional nature. 'I became anxious about marriage', she told me, 'when we finally fixed the day for it. I suppose I realized then for the first time what a great step it is. Oh, I was sure enough of my love for Robert and of his for me. There were none of those doubts — as to whether we were suited for each other, that is. Nothing like that, for we are always so happy together. And it is so good to know that both our families are behind us too.'

She went on to explain how the same night after their wedding plans were announced she had slept restlessly. This, she was sure, was due to excitement. The next morning, the skin rash had appeared and gradually got worse. 'I suppose', she said, 'it is because I am so concerned about my skin clearing up in time that I have become more and more worked up about it as our wedding day approaches.

31

Yet though I know that nervous tension is the cause I just cannot calm myself. Every night I hope the rash will have gone by morning, but now I am quite frantic about it being still there on the day.'

'You are right', I replied. 'Worrying about it so much prevents it from recovering. However, you know about spiritual healing and its fundamental purpose of creating a calm and confident spirit. Involved as you are now with all the preparation for your wedding it is doubly difficult for you to relax enough to discover interior stillness. Quite often our days can be likened to a whirlwind, an exercise of tremendous activity. Nevertheless at the centre, as with the whirlwind, there should be complete calm. Life ought to be like that, full of energy, but we should always hold on to quietness deep within ourselves. We will seek that centre now with all the confidence and assurance which it gives. First, then, let us be silent for a while and think only of stillness. It will probably help if you imagine that you are gazing upon the quiet surface of a pond — no movement at all, just tranquillity. Take my hand and we will think of this together.'

At first her hand felt tense in mine, and though I had asked her to lean back comfortably in an easy chair I could tell that her body was taut and nervous. I spoke no more and let my mind dwell upon the thought of stillness in the symbol I had suggested to her. I conjured a mental picture of myself standing motionless beside a lake and gazing upon its unruffled waters.

Next I thought of Jesus. Soon he appeared to be standing beside me. Our reflection, his and mine, upon the water looked solid and real. By a further concentration I summoned the girl into the picture as well. Now she and I were standing on either side of Jesus, and our images were there upon the serene surface. There was a strange quality about the picture. Often when we are among a group which is looking in a mirror it is the reflection of ourselves which dominates and holds our special attention. But in this picture it was the figure of Christ which stood out. After a while those of the young woman and of myself seemed to merge into his. The picture had become an illustration of our mystical union with Christ. Now we were one in him.

People have said to me that seeing Jesus in this way is purely a figment of the imagination, and some would therefore dismiss this mental exercise as without value. No one can envisage, they say, what he is like in his transcendence or what he looked like on this earth two thousand years ago. But the use of the mind to create a picture within it of Jesus is, I believe, of enormous help, perhaps even essential, if we are to realize his presence with us. That picture may be one associated with the traditional representations of him in art or, as in my own case here, of no greater detail than the outline of a white-robed figure. But whatever our imagination does about this the fact remains that the mental picture we summon up is invested with reality by the eye of faith. We are thus truly seeing him who is invisible. Christianity is the religion of the incarnation, and so it is wholly legitimate to bring before our mind's eye the actual presence of our Lord in this way. Indeed I believe it is the only way for most people to begin at all along the mystic path.

But to return to my narrative. During the moment of mystical union the words of Jesus came to me: 'Peace I leave with you. My peace I give to you.' At this point I felt the young woman's hand go limp. It seemed to become fused with my own. I looked at her; her eyes were closed and I could sense that she had at last truly relaxed. 'Lord Jesus,' I said quietly, 'may thy peace come upon us and enter the soul of this child of thine. Take from her now all her stress and anxiety. Let her know only the tranquillity of thy presence. In this hour, dear Lord, she comes to thee for thy healing.'

The quiet which followed had an exquisite quality which I felt had enveloped us with a strange, vibrant energy. I recalled the analogy of the whirlwind. All around

33

us was a sublime and tremendous power but at the centre, as it were, we shared an oasis of perfect calm. The symbol had become the reality.

At last the peculiar beauty of this experience faded, and I became conscious once more of my study and its furniture and, finally, of my physical body. The trance had ended. I glanced at the young woman. She too appeared to be emerging from a state of trance. When she opened her eyes she shook her head a little as if adjusting to full consciousness. As I let go her hand she said softly: 'Thank you so much. I feel so calm now. I don't think I have ever felt so peaceful before in all my life.' We returned to the room where her mother was being entertained by my wife. 'Diana will be perfectly all right in time for the wedding', I told her.

Soon after the wedding she wrote to say that her daughter's complaint had completely cleared. All traces had vanished on the morning after the girl had been to see me. 'It was like a miracle,' she wrote, 'and on the day of her wedding Diana looked so radiant and happy. She told me that she had come away after seeing you last week so buoyant that she was certain everything would now be well for her. "You have no idea, Mother", she said, "the wonderful sense of peace I experienced." '

7

PEACE AT THE LAST

The benefit of the laying-on of hands is not confined to physical illness. In cases of anxiety, depression, or melancholy it can be especially helpful by assuring people that they are not adrift on a sea of uncaring and impersonal fate, but that there is love and understanding at the heart of things, and the continuing hope of a renewal of their life and purpose.

A woman parishioner came to me in great concern about a teenage girl whose mother had been taken to hospital. As the father was elderly, the mother was worried that he could not properly care for the girl. When I went to see the mother in hospital she immediately recognized me as her vicar although I had never met her before. 'I have been so worried', she said. 'There has been something on my mind for years; I have so often wanted to come and see you about it but have always put it off.'

'Perhaps I can help you', I replied. 'I understand your daughter is the problem. Is that so?' 'Oh, no, not the way some are these days', she answered. 'She is a very good girl. Her father is very old, of course. Much older than I am. And perhaps he can't be very helpful to her. But she is not a trouble to either of us. It's nothing like that.' She paused and looked away from me. I felt she needed encouraging. 'Then what can it be?' I asked gently. 'What is the worry? You know you can tell me whatever it is in confidence.'

After a while she turned her face towards me again though her eyes were still downcast. 'It's me', she said, breaking the silence at last. 'I'm no good, you see. I've done a very wicked thing.' 'Well, whatever it is,' I said, 'if you know it is wrong and are sorry about it, God will forgive you.'

'He can't forgive what I have done', she declared, and began to cry. 'There is nothing he does not forgive', I hastened to say. 'Of that I am quite sure. But what is it? Can you tell me about it? It often helps to talk to someone about one's worries.'

She looked most pitiable. A frail creature nervously plucking the bedclothes, too weak to wipe away her tears. A long silence followed and I prayed inwardly that she would be given the courage to confide in me so that I might be able to offer help or guidance. Finally she spoke, this time looking directly at me. 'I did a dreadful thing', she said. 'For twenty years we have been living together, but we couldn't ever marry. You see he has a wife. I know it is a dreadful sin — and there's my daughter. God can't forgive me. It's too late.'

I did my best to pacify her and repeated several times that what she had done was not so terrible a thing. Clearly she had been brought up in a very stern way with no idea of God as merciful, only as some unrelenting judge. I endeavoured to leave her with an easier conscience. At last, by continued reassurance, I thought the idea of the understanding and forgiving love of Jesus Christ had begun to pierce the hard crust of her childhood's religious training. She even managed a smile by the time I left her.

But two later visits I made showed that she was still dwelling on the enormity of her 'sin'. She was firmly convinced that she was going to face an implacable God. At the end of each of those visits I only succeeded in leaving her somewhat less morbid than when I arrived. The mental agony was clearly still there. The Sister on the ward, too, was now showing great concern about her patient's melancholy and her constant reference to the anger of God for her having lived 'in sin' for so many years.

A call I made on the man did not prove very helpful either. He seemed past any comprehension of the tragedy, quite unable to appreciate that this woman who had lived faithfully with him for twenty years and had borne him a child was suffering so cruelly. No one could make him see that a kindly visit from him might have given the poor soul some consolation. I suppose he was just too old to care, although he was perfectly able to attend the hospital and, though in his late eighties, actually still drove his car.

During the week it had been made clear to me by the doctor that her death could now only be a few days away. The next time I went to the hospital I knew I must break through this dreadful cloud of ignorance and make positive to her the shining beauty of the love of God. As I set out I felt absolutely sure it was now or never, and throughout the journey by Underground I concentrated on the problem. I asked God to bring relief to her tortured mind and prayed that he would use me this very day to bring to her the illumination of his compassion.

Again I was standing by her bed. She lifted her hand to me. This act seemed to take all her strength. She was obviously at a very low ebb. I took it in mine and remained holding it as I spoke to her. She was clearly glad to see me, but within moments she showed she was still preoccupied with the old worry. She brought the subject up herself. So once more I went over, but very briefly this time, some of the well trodden paths of my former visits. I pictured for her again some of the glowing examples of the understanding and infinite pity of Jesus. But still, though she listened with what seemed rapt attention, she went on in the same old strain. Clearly she was not convinced that in her case there could be either mercy or forgiveness. But this time I knew intuitively that the special grace of the laying-on of hands would bring the assurance required. I did not feel one whit dismayed, therefore, by her despondent attitude.

'Do you remember', I asked, 'that Jesus and his disciples laid their hands on people and they were healed?' She nodded. 'Sometimes', I continued, 'those people were ones who needed healing for their minds because they were troubled about wrong things they had done. Do you think he would have healed them too?'

37

'Of course,' she said, 'because he loved all of them alike.' I felt a certain satisfaction at this, because she was repeating an actual phrase I had often used during my previous visits.

'So, you see, he will forgive you also, absolutely. We will ask him to do that now.' Immediately I placed my hands on her head. She closed her eyes. Almost it seemed to me she knew what was coming for her tenseness left her in that moment. 'Jesus, we know you love everyone no matter what they have done. Lay your loving hands on this child of yours who is so deeply and truly sorry for her sin, and forgive her now.'

As my hands remained on her head I pictured Jesus standing with the two of us. The picture became clearer, and I saw him lay his hands tenderly upon this poor dying woman whose wasted form lay there so weak, so helpless, needing only one more thing in this life, the knowledge of God's forgiveness. I knew in that moment she had received it. And I sensed that now, at last, she knew it too.

'Our heavenly Father has forgiven you, my dear', I said. Her face, which had become so tiny in the past few weeks through devastating illness, looked as if the sunshine had fallen upon it, despite the grey, overcast sky of that wintry afternoon. She was no longer restless. Her frail, almost transparent hands had ceased their nervous screwing of the sheets and lay still. 'I know', she said. 'He has forgiven me, because he loves me.'

Then she lay back, quite relaxed, upon the pillows. 'God bless you and keep you', I said. At this she opened her eyes for a second and smiled as if fully content. As I moved away to leave the ward I thought I heard her speaking, and so I quickly returned to her bedside. She looked as if she were asleep and at last quite peaceful. She was murmuring to herself and I had to bend low to hear: 'Jesus has forgiven me because he loves me. Oh, thank you, Jesus. Thank you, thank you for loving me. Jesus has forgiven me because he loves me. Oh, thank you, Jesus, thank you for loving me.' She was repeating this still when I finally left her.

As I went back through the hospital I was almost overwhelmed with a great sense of relief. My whole being was suddenly filled with new joy and zest and was so wonderfully uplifted that I could hardly believe I was still in this world. Outside the grim, grey buildings and rain-soaked pavements of London appeared gloomy no longer. Because my heart was light, now that God's love had become known to her through the laying-on of hands, the world was radiant too. It was not just the lifting of a spiritual burden which had in these sad weeks oppressed me, but rather its complete dissolution. I was not with her when she died two days later, but the Sister of the ward specially asked to see me when I called again at the hospital.

'I felt I must tell you what a wonderful and peaceful end it was', she said. 'You know how anxious we all were about her terribly sad delusion of being totally unworthy of God's forgiveness. At times it was so pathetic even we nurses could have cried. Nothing, it seemed, could help, and we know how much you tried. Well, on the day you laid your hands on her head everything changed. She was like a different person. She took my hand every time I went to see her and would say: "Sister, it's wonderful. Jesus loves me. And I am forgiven. Don't worry any more about me. I shall be going after all to the heavenly Father's home. Now I am happy at last. Remember, Sister, God loves us all." '

8

THE LAYING-ON OF HANDS

I am often asked whether I use a special technique when administering the laying-on of hands. The answer is that I have never consciously used a set form. Each case seems to vary, and the approach I feel drawn to make usually differs in some particular. In the early days of my ministry, I would lay my hands on the person's head or shoulders. However, I came to realize that actual contact was necessary only for a few moments at the start or sometimes not at all. As regards psychic phenomena, about which I am also often asked, there are physical sensations which I find are still quite marked when my hands are several inches away. I have even known this 'influence' to continue perceptibly several feet away from the outline of the body. It is as if I am contacting an invisible aura.

These sensations usually include a tingling like pins and needles developing sometimes to a strong tremor in my hands. Often I notice a pronounced heat being generated. The intensity of these phenomena may increase to a degree where they appear to affect my whole body. On some occasions it is as if my feet have risen from the ground or as if the upper part of my body has been cut off at the waist, leaving the lower part devoid of all feeling. It is, I suppose, similar to levitation. Usually I gradually raise my hands further away from the person's head. It is difficult to describe some of the sensations. At times it is as if there were tiny chains connecting my fingers and palms to the person through which a kind of energy pulses at great speed.

At the end of the administration I usually find myself describing with my hands a complete circle around the person, who may be kneeling or sitting while I am standing in front. I do this by touching the tips of my fingers behind the head and then bringing them round, at a radius of a foot or so, until they meet in front of the forehead. All the while the vibration usually continues at a perceptible level. Afterwards I often find myself flicking my fingers or drawing my hands through each other as if removing some alien substance from them. It could, I suppose, be described as a type of ritual washing but it is quite involuntary. It certainly seems as if I am obeying something instinctive which I do not consciously understand. In fact I often have the marked sense of acting under the influence of a power beyond my own, and beyond my understanding. Nevertheless, I do not feel that my own individuality has been lost but rather that this power comes to raise it, for the time being, into a realm beyond space and time. Indeed, at those times I can appreciate such expressions as 'out of the body' and 'transcendental experience'.

I have said that there is usually a sense of heat. In an endeavour to rationalize this I have tried to view it in as detached a way as I can while I am experiencing it. I have noted that the warmth is always concentrated on the underside of the hands. There have been times when I have visited a sick person and observed that my hands were bitterly cold at the start, having just come in from wintry conditions outdoors. When I have conducted the administration near a good fire, I have thought that that is the reason for the heat in my hands, only to realize that the backs of them were directed towards the blaze and were still very cold. The palms, however, which were screened from its heat by being above the person, were tingling with warmth. I must underline that none of these phenomena occurs automatically. They come only when prayer has been made. Normally this is offered only after I have first reminded the invalid of God's love for him or her.

There are times when I experience the reverse sensation.

Instead of heat there is a drop in temperature, even to the extent of a definite chill. Often in these cases I have found that the patient has been suffering from some sort of mental disorder or has recently been dosed with drugs to allay pain or remove anxiety. This coldness is also manifested when the person is in a condition of final coma.

In the latter case I sense that the body before me is already empty of its spirit-soul. It is virtually a corpse, even though death may not be pronounced until hours, or even days later. I do not doubt, however, that the spirit-soul may return briefly from time to time to the body during a lengthy unconsciousness before final death. This, I believe, is the reason for the sense that comes to me most strongly by the bedside of persons whose dying is very prolonged, of being acutely conscious sometimes of what I can only describe as 'an emptiness', and at other times of a very real presence in the dying body.

On some occasions when I have had this strong impression of emptiness I have been aware of an unseen being who is either just beside me, or right behind me. This could, I believe, be the soul of that dying person, the soul of a welcoming and predeceased loved one, or an angelic being. But it might be the spirit-soul of a living relative or friend. I surmise this last possibility because someone praying earnestly for the dying beloved may, albeit unconsciously, convey his or her spirit-soul to the bedside. The intensity of such prayer can be particularly profound by those who, perhaps only a little while before, have visited the sickroom or hospital. The picture they carry away of that person they love makes it highly likely that when they return to the quiet of their homes they will mentally transport themselves to that bedside in their pure abandon in heartfelt prayer.

I believe I have had confirmation of this theory on a number of occasions when I have visited hospitals and sensed most strongly a benign presence while I prayed with patients. Afterwards I have learned that a close relative had visited the sick person only a few minutes before my arrival and had then gone to the hospital chapel where he or she had engaged in fervent prayer during the very period of my visit. In such cases I believe the spirit-soul of the relative was transported to the bedside, and my own concentrated state of prayer had made me peculiarly aware of it.

One of the loveliest features of the laying-on of hands is the wonderful tranquillity which concludes its administration. During it I feel I am in the presence of great spiritual power, and there is a buoyant feeling of assurance. Afterwards I usually experience a drowsiness for an hour or so, as if vital forces within me have been expended. At times I find I must sit down or remain kneeling quietly for a little while. But when the fatigue departs I receive such a flood of well-being and contentment that the aftermath of administration is best described as one of elation.

Another phenomenon which sometimes accompanies my laying-on of hands is the manifestation of light. A better description would be 'radiance'. In such cases dark rooms appear to be suffused with light which can range from a gentle golden luminosity to a dazzling brilliance. Even with my eyes closed I can see this light just as strongly. It is not a case of the delayed image such as one gets after concentration upon a lamp or lighted window. More often than not I try to ensure that my back is towards any such illumination and so there is no retained image. Rather it is that the room itself seems to be illumined. This light often comes quite suddenly. I can only describe it as unearthly, because it has a quality which is unlike either natural or artificial light.

At times I have observed a light about the person during my ministration. This is a soft, glowing radiance usually about the head. I can quite understand, therefore, that the halo so often depicted in religious paintings is not a fiction but represents a true spiritual experience. There have been some occasions when I have observed this glow about the whole person as a kind of enveloping aura.

When visiting someone who is in bed I find that I may be impelled to start the laying-on of hands close to the crown of the head and the brow but then include the full length of the recumbent body. In this event I move my hands back and forth at a distance of about twelve inches above the person. This movement I have found is akin to stroking, as if soothing and calming. In the course of this I have sometimes noticed that my hands will feel a definite build-up of heat over an area which is causing pain or where the particular affliction is located.

One example concerns a friend whom I had not seen for several years. His wife telephoned me to ask if I would visit him, as he was ill and had asked to see me. It was on a Christmas Eve and so I suggested that my visit should include giving him his Christmas Communion. On arriving at his bedside I told him that I would administer the laying-on of hands after he had received the sacrament. He expressed deep gratitude at this and said he had been hoping I would do so as he knew that I practiced it. He was obviously very concerned about his condition. He was a highly intelligent, middle-aged man with a responsible job, not at all the kind of person who could in any sense be thought either superstitious or impressionable.

In passing my hands above him I noticed an intense heat rising from his abdomen. With both hands a few inches above this area I continued with gentle stroking movements until the heat appeared to diminish. His eyes were closed when I said to him: 'This is where the pain is.' I was neither touching him nor had he seen where my hands were at this juncture. Yet his reply was quick and positive: 'Yes, Padre, that is it – but it's gone, this very moment.' He opened his eyes and had such a look of thankfulness and serenity, so different from the worried, anxious look before, that I found myself with tears filling my own as I gave thanks to God for his healing. It later transpired that he had had a severe stomach ulcer which, from then on, ceased to cause him further trouble. At the time he had suspected his pain was due to something more sinister, as he had lately lost a near relative and several friends through cancer.

Although I do not always make or maintain physical contact during the laying-on of hands, yet I can usually feel a gathering firmness beneath my hands as if I am touching a solid substance. I can only liken this to the resilient feeling which a sponge gives. I sense a positive resistance if I press downwards against it with my hands. Intuitively I realize I must only caress, as it were, this strange emanation rising from the person's body. I know that unless I break from my semi-trance condition it is impossible for me to bring my hands down through this peculiar barrier.

For me this is evidence that there is an aura, possibly electrical, which shrouds our physical bodies and which, perhaps, is affected by illness or disease. It is, I believe, an attribute of the soul. I also believe that our own aura cannot break through that of someone else, just as our physical bodies remain separate even in the closest union of human relationship. But each aura can, I am sure, influence the other for good or ill, according to our willing. This gives some measure of proof to the Christian belief that the soul has an individuality which cannot be totally absorbed by another.

Other faiths assert that the soul must be taken up into the divine essence like a drop of water to be lost in the great ocean. Christians believe, however, that the soul has an immortal personality and its highest good, willed by its Creator, is for it to reach the bliss of fulfilment, not that it should be absorbed and lost in him. The divine nature revealed by Christ is love, and it is the nature of love to have an object to love, not to end its being by consuming its object.

I have noted the phenomenon of transfiguration more often when there has first been a celebration of Holy Communion for the sick person. It occurs particularly in the case of elderly people. The countenance appears luminous and the skin, while very white, suggests not pallor but an attractive vitality which is difficult to describe. Again the only adjective is 'unearthly'. All lines of age, pain, or tension appear to vanish and the face seems young, though this also is a word that does not do real justice to the change. The serenity that comes, for example, to a face that is deeply careworn is wonderfully beautiful. The person usually remains quite still and silent for some moments afterwards as if savouring a delight of supreme pleasure which he or she is reluctant to lose and which is not of this world. The atmosphere is charged with the peculiar energy of a great peace.

I recall a schoolmistress, greatly loved by her pupils, who had been taken suddenly to hospital. I only received news of this a few days later and called to see her. I had been told her condition was extremely serious though I did not know what the exact trouble was. Before I went into the ward the Sister told me that she was very weak and to be prepared for the fact that most probably she would be unaware of my presence.

I stood at her side for some moments and began to pray silently for her. Then an inner voice told me that I must think especially of her heart. The voice continued to prompt me. I took her hand, which was lying limply on the coverlet, gently between my two hands. Then I tried to become aware of the beat of my own heart and prayed that God would transfer, as it were, the steadiness of my pulse to hers.

After a little while I became conscious of the pulse throbbing in my hands. They seemed to have fused with her hand so that our life force had become one. We were in the mighty embrace of the supreme life of God and it was his power which coursed through me, through my hands and into her. The rhythm of its flow felt steady and controlled, and after a while I could distinctly feel an even response from her own pulse. At first it had been so faint that I could not distinguish it at all. Now the beat was as steady and distinct as my own. I continued to maintain the thought of St Paul: 'In God we live and move and have our being.' I made the text come alive by asserting over and over the thought of God as Father and the two of us as his children. I reminded myself also that Jesus Christ was present.

I remained as motionless as possible, not wishing to disturb her, for she appeared to be in a deep sleep. There was a strange stillness about the bed. Then she suddenly opened her eyes and saw me. With a sweet smile she said: 'Thank you so much for coming to see me.' 'I have just been praying for you', I replied. 'I know that you have', she said, and there was a look of understanding in her eyes which made me realize that though my prayer had been silent she had, none the less, been aware of it at the deep level of the spirit.

Now I leaned forward and placed my right hand above her forehead and my left above her chest. My fingers began to quiver slightly as if a current of electricity were passing through them. I concentrated on bringing them under steady control as if to soothe with gentleness. I prayed again, this time aloud: 'Lord Jesus, present now in all thy power, and in whom we have all trust, lay thy hands of healing upon this thy child.'

She had closed her eyes again and there was a look of deep relief and relaxation upon her face. 'You have received great healing', I said at length. These words came as if their source were the very air around us. They did not seem to be my own at all but uttered without conscious thought on my part. I believe I had for these moments become a channel which was in contact with a mysterious energy. Her reply was to nod quietly. Then she opened her eyes again. In them I saw the light of a great assurance. It was movingly beautiful.

When I left her I was surprised by the strength of her grip on my hand as I took hers to say goodbye. It was as if through that grip she was conveying to me her conviction

47

that she had received a great blessing and was expressing her profound thanksgiving for it. The following day I learned that during the night of my visit to her the crisis had passed and that she was on the road to recovery.

9

FROM BEYOND DEATH

Certain phenomena are associated particularly with death or the imminence of it. Early in my ministry I was asked to visit a dying woman. Her sister had sent for me, and as I followed her upstairs to the bedroom it seemed to me that someone passed me going downstairs. I instinctively moved to one side, and although I could see nothing my reaction was quite natural and spontaneous.

Obviously I was absorbed in the purpose of my visit; nevertheless I was very conscious that whoever, or whatever, had passed me was of a reassuring nature. There was nothing spooky about it. In fact I had a sudden feeling of great confidence, almost of elation. From that moment my perplexity as to what I must say or do in the sick-room completely vanished. I should mention here that on almost every occasion when I have to go into the presence of sickness or sorrow I experience just beforehand a daunting sense of concern, almost of trepidation, about what action I must take or be prepared for.

The dying woman had been unconscious for over two days, and when I stood bỹ the bed I looked down on a form which was quite inert save for the heavy breathing of coma. Without hesitation, but not really knowing why I did so, I took the limp hand lying on the coverlet and then, stooping down, spoke closely into her ear. Again my action was unpremeditated. It was as if I were being guided automatically. Gently I whispered, 'God bless you.' The response was immediate, though of the briefest. This woman, who had been in a condition of coma for more than forty-eight hours, and who was never to speak again before she died, opened her eyes and said, quite distinctly, 'He *has* blessed me.' When she had said this her eyes closed again and the stertorous breathing recommenced.

I have often thought about this matter since and asked myself who passed me on those stairs and seemed to be coming away even as I was going to that death-bed. Could it have been the dying woman's guardian angel who had given her some special and beautiful reassurance? Or was it, perhaps, a former loved one who, from the world of spirit, had greeted her for her journey into that same new world? Or had indeed the spirit-soul of this woman already found some liberation from her dying physical body?

Who can say what this strange experience really was or its full significance? All I can do is to record the fact of it and underline once more the naturalness and joyousness which accompanied it. At the time it felt the most normal thing in the world, as if the presence of death ought to have this kind of feeling about it.

Another phenomenon associated with death occurred when I was serving as a chaplain in the Royal Air Force. My wife and I lived for a time in a charming manor house, part Elizabethan, with windows overlooking the ancient parish church. The atmosphere of the house seemed to breathe all the peace and beauty of the country together with the sense of many associations with the church through the centuries. I mention this because I think it has a bearing on the incident I now relate. For I believe that some buildings can assist in the manifestation of psychic phenomena, more especially if they are old and situated near churches or burial grounds, or on former sites of them.

One night I awoke to see a form standing at the foot of our bed. I felt no sense of surprise or unease and immediately recognized the figure of my brother. He was a naval officer who had died at the age of thirty-six, about six years before. He was looking at me in the most cheerful and reassuring way. Though I did not hear any voice, I sensed that he wished to let me know that he was very happy.

I could see that he was in naval uniform, though I was

only clearly aware of one arm. On the sleeve were the gold rings of his naval rank. This manifestation lasted only a few seconds, but the impression created was very vivid and uplifting. It gave me such pleasure that I felt I wanted to wake my wife and tell her about it. But it was very early in the morning so I decided to say nothing. However, later that week I mentioned it to her and she said she too that same night had woken and become vividly aware of my brother's presence. She also had noted the uniform sleeve markings and had sensed the great cheerfulness of his presence, just as he had had in his lifetime. She had found the experience, even as I had done, one of tremendous reassurance.

Our sharing of this incident in detail and with similar reactions was probably another instance of that telepathy which exists between us. What is more remarkable is that neither of us had recently been talking or thinking about my brother. All I can say is that we both shared the experience and found it greatly comforting. There was no prepared state of mind in either of us and certainly no conscious desire for it. It just happened.

Some years later another such experience occurred when I was engrossed in writing a sermon. I was completely alone in the vicarage, as my wife was at the church arranging the altar flowers. She too was on her own. The time was about 6 p.m. and my study was becoming rather dark.

I was putting the finishing touches to my writing when I heard the front door of the vicarage open and someone enter the hall. The person seemed to hesitate for a moment outside my study door and then, as I assumed, went into the room opposite which we used as a dining-room. I presumed that my wife must have returned from church. I called out a greeting but received no answer. For a few minutes I took no further notice as I wished to finish what I was doing. But then I wondered why she had neither replied nor come into my study, as she would normally do directly she arrived home.

Consequently I came from my study into the entrance hall. It was empty and the light had not been switched on. Mystified, I called out again but there was no answer. So positive was I that she must have come into the house (no one else could have done so because only she and I had keys) that I went all over the large vicarage looking for her. I was absolutely convinced that someone had entered the house. It was natural to believe it must be my wife. Indeed, when I had first left my study I could have sworn that there was the sense of a person having recently been in the hall. The house just did not feel empty.

Eventually I decided to go down to the church, which stood in a neighbouring road. By this time I must confess I was rather annoyed, thinking my wife's little joke, as I felt sure it must be, was overdone. Sure enough she was in the church. I asked her why she had come back to the vicarage only to leave it again without letting me know or even responding to my greeting when I heard her come in. At this she looked quite blank. 'But I haven't been back', she said. 'As you can see I still haven't finished here with the flowers.'

Although now convinced that she had not returned I argued a little because my impression that someone had opened the front door and entered the house was still very strong. The whole affair was extremely puzzling although the actual experience of hearing the doors open and close, and the sense of someone pausing outside my study, had not felt the least bit strange or disturbing at the time.

Needless to say all was quiet and in order when we returned together. We thought little more about this incident until the following Monday when I learned from the headmistress of our Church School, who had seen the announcement in the obituary column of *The Times*, that a former vicar of my parish had died. Later I was to discover that his death had actually occurred within half an hour of my unaccountable visit at the vicarage.

Further details emerged in due course which convinced me that his spirit-soul had returned to the vicarage. Only a month or so before his death he and his wife had revisited the parish to look up some old friends. He spoke to us of the great delight he always had in the vicarage garden with its fine fruit trees. He also said that his years as vicar of the parish had been among the happiest of his ministry and that the vicarage itself was also greatly loved by him and his family. Furthermore the room he had used for interviewing parishioners, and as a study, was the one we used for a dining-room. As I have said, this was the very room which I believed the visitant had entered after pausing momentarily in the hallway.

I am led to believe, therefore, that my predecessor had, soon after his death, journeyed happily and naturally back to where he had enjoyed so much his life and ministry on earth. In the gathering twilight and in the depth of my concentration upon my sermon I would have been verging on a state of controlled trance, making the consciousness of my body minimal. In that state I would be especially open to the awareness of another spirit-soul.

My wife and I for several weeks thereafter would hear what seemed to be the front door clicking open and the sound as of someone entering the hall passage and then pausing as if to enter one of the rooms. This phenomenon was always so convincingly natural that every time it happened to either of us each would go into the hall to see if it were the other who had returned from some errand. On many occasions my wife had this experience about 11.30 a.m. on a Thursday morning. In consequence she would call out from the kitchen, thinking that I had returned from the celebration of Holy Communion which I took every Thursday at 11 a.m. Often she would leave the kitchen where she would be busy preparing lunch and come into the hall expecting to speak to me, only to find that no one was there. The service would have ended about 11.30 a.m., but I could not get back to the house

53

until about a quarter of an hour later.

I began to believe that my dead predecessor wished to be present at this service, one which he would have celebrated regularly, even as I was now doing, on that same day of the week and at the same hour, for such had been the tradition for many years. This belief was reinforced when one day no communicants arrived to share the service with me. Nevertheless I read it through to myself. I had just started the Consecration Prayer when I suddenly felt that someone was present. In consequence, thinking it must be a late comer, I began to read the prayer aloud. On turning my back to the altar I saw for a fleeting moment a figure, with head bowed in its hands, kneeling in the front pew. Involuntarily I stretched out my hand towards it in welcome, and immediately it dissolved before I could recognize it. I must have been in some degree of trance at the time owing to deep concentration upon the reading of the service. My movement, because it made me more conscious of my body, would have broken this state. In consequence my spirit-soul faculties would have been impaired and the apparition would have vanished.

These visitations to the vicarage were never unpleasant, and we came to the conclusion that there was a little haunting, of a happy and even comforting kind, going on. Perhaps because we mentioned the matter to several friends, this phenomenon ceased after about six weeks. I feel there is nothing untoward or unseemly in the view that after death the spirit-soul may instinctively desire to visit for a while, in its new-found freedom, those places which were of deep significance and special delight during the earth life. Then, as I believe, comes the fuller acceptance and appreciation of the richer horizon of life now open to it in the transcendent world. Thus follows the willing and grateful relinquishment of all earthbound experience.

10

A CLOUD OF GLORY

A most disturbing psychic experience was associated not with natural but with violent death. It concerned the funeral of a father and his two children which I had to conduct. The father, in a condition of great mental darkness, had murdered his young son and daughter. On my way to the cemetery I was so preoccupied with the need to formulate some suitable prayers which would convey special understanding and comfort to his wife, the children's mother, that I was quite literally in a daze when I crossed a busy road. As a result I was nearly knocked down by a car when I stepped off the kerb. But even this did not entirely jolt me out of my concentrated thought.

I conducted the first part of the funeral service in the chapel, but owing to sudden and torrential rain which waterlogged the grave it was not possible to carry out the actual interment and committal until the next day.

When the father's coffin first passed me in the chapel I perceived a sense of great sadness, so profound that the very air seemed heavy with it. When the little white coffin of the older child was brought in I had no special feeling except one of great personal sorrow. But when the third tiny coffin of the little boy was carried in I was suddenly gripped by the most desolating atmosphere of shock and horror which appeared to be wrapped around it. Indeed the psychic feeling generated was so intense that I thought I would be physically sick. In one fleeting and awful moment I thought I could actually see through the wood of the coffin the frail form within. I could not control the shudders of emotion which shook me from head to foot. How I maintained any composure at all or succeeded in completing the service I do not know.

The bodies remained in the chapel throughout that night due to the sudden deluge, and the following day I conducted their committal. For this completion of the funeral service no one else was present except the officials involved.

When I entered the chapel to escort the coffins to the grave I sensed again the depressing anguish of the day before. I had hoped that because the bodies had rested through the night in the calm and holy peace of the chapel this would have been dispelled. I had thought much about the matter during the night and prayed about it. Now I stood for a little while before the altar praying that the Father would grant his mercy and blessing to the distraught soul of the man and provide the beautiful promise of eternity to all three victims. After this prayer I felt that the grimness of the atmosphere was somewhat lessened.

The final ordeal was still to come. The solemn cortège of coffin-bearers followed me across the cemetery to the grave. As we went I prayed silently over and over again for the peace and fulfilment of these three souls. On the faces of the undertakers and grave-diggers were the expressions of the deepest emotion. I had never seen the like at any funeral before.

Overwhelmed as I had been by the tragic agony of the affair hitherto, yet during the three committals into one grave I was suddenly filled with the most sublime relief. All care and confusion departed from me and I was filled with pure content. Through the mist of tears which had come to my eyes while I watched the coffins being lowered and saw the distress of all those around the grave, I suddenly noticed what appeared to be a very bright light which hovered above the coffins. This gradually rose up and expanded into an umbrella-shaped cloud of golden glory which enveloped me and that sad little group of men. It remained thus for several seconds after I had completed the words of the committal, and I found deep comfort in it.

I am sure that this was purely a subjective experience. Certainly none of those grouped around the grave ever mentioned it to me. But though they may not have witnessed it I am certain that they shared with me that accompanying sense of peace and consolation when the service by the graveside was over. To me that vision was a sure token and seal of God's all-embracing love, taking away completely all the anguish and horror which had been so pervasive until then.

Later I was able to gather greater details of this tragedy. The father, in the distress of his unbalanced mind, had taken a revolver and shot his elder child in the back of the head while she sat at a table busily occupied in drawing and painting. She had died instantly and completely unaware. The younger child, however, shocked by the noise of the gun, ran about the room in terror. Finally he was shot while crouching under a sideboard to hide away. Then the demented father had turned the weapon upon himself.

I then realized why my reactions to the three coffins had been what they were. From the moment I heard of the tragedy the responsibility of how to convey to the bereaved relatives and friends the consolation which only trust in God's compassion and understanding can provide had weighed most heavily upon me. I had spent a great deal of time composing special prayers and a short address for the funeral service. For three days I was preoccupied with these considerations, and two nights were restless with them.

A period of such concentration, by blotting out almost every other matter, had practically induced a state of trance. Hence my inattentive crossing of that busy road and my susceptibility to psychic forces. I believe, and I think this particular experience lends support to my view, that the strong psychic forces which are engendered by grievous shock or violent emotions will cling for some time in the area where they have been aroused and perhaps become temporarily attached, as in this case, to a corpse.

11

IN THE LEE OF A CHURCH

I have come to believe that some places stimulate extra-sensory perception more than others, perhaps even foster it. I am convinced, for example, that churches in particular are liable to produce psychic experience in those who spend most of their working lives in or around them, or whose homes are nearby. To this I can testify from numerous experiences I have had while living in houses near a church. Others, too, have told me of phenomena they have known when they have lived or worked near ancient churches or old burial grounds.

Sometimes my wife has shared my experiences. The reason for this would seem to be that the years together have made us, like many married couples, highly telepathic with each other. Hence, although the psychic experience may have initially been mine it would almost instantly be apprehended by her as well.

One September I was performing the duties of a locum-tenens for the chaplain of the English Church at Nice in the south of France. During this period my wife and I stayed at the chaplain's house, which is close to the church. One night I awoke suddenly from a sound sleep and my wife did the same just a moment later. There seemed no particular reason for this, no loud or unusual sound.

On first waking I told her that 'I felt I was not in Nice but back in our London vicarage. My wife said she felt the same. Then followed the strong impression that something very unpleasant was taking place there. It is significant to mention that this vicarage is also close to the church. Indeed it is partially integrated with it.

We had always been concerned about leaving the vicarage

empty for any long period because on several unforgettable occasions burglary had been attempted and only foiled because we were in the house each time, although our presence was unknown to the would-be intruders until we surprised them. It was probably natural, therefore, that we should suppose that something of this kind was now taking place at our home. However, the intensity of our impression was such that we were convinced it was no mere imagining. Something wrong was surely going on.

There was only one thing we could do in the circumstances, and that was to make a prayer for the protection of our property. At the same time I tried an experiment. I relaxed as much as my anxiety would permit. Then I sought to project my spirit-soul across the continent to Hampstead. In my mind's eye I created a precise picture of the vicarage and, through this, 'transported' us to our bedroom in it.

Then a strange thing began to happen. The actual construction of the mental picture seemed to be taken out of my own control and was being completed for me. A scene manifested itself, although imprecisely, in which we were first investigating, and finally actually defending our home from what appeared to be some kind of depredation by two men. Vague as the details were, one item appeared clearly: a car was involved in some way. Everything ended by my restraining the two men, but how I did so was not clear. Eventually they took to their heels.

My mental exercise in all this had taken several minutes. During that period I experienced an increasing tension, culminating at last in a veritable tussle of will in which I felt the strain of trying to maintain my projected presence. Prayer for divine protection, however, brought great relief and reassurance which was succeeded by a feeling of elation, as if some conflict had been successfully resolved. I took note of the time. It was around midnight.

When we returned to England three weeks later we learned that about that time that same night two men had entered the forecourt of the vicarage. As parking facilities in the area are at a premium, we allow a neighbour to park her car in our forecourt. The two men had attempted to steal it. It was clear that they had made various efforts to open it, finally breaking a door handle but still failing to get inside. Next they tried to push it into the road. Evidently they had had a struggle to do this, as their strongly marked footprints were everywhere. Again they had been thwarted because the car jammed against one of the gateposts. They abandoned it with its bonnet and front wheels protruding through the gates of the drive. Presumably out of frustration, they smashed the headlamps before they left.

The date, the time, and other accurate details of the strange awareness which I had of all this in Nice could have been just coincidence. We were certain, however, that this was not so because our impression of something being amiss had been vivid to the point of reality. Was my attempt to exercise influence from afar one of the factors which helped to foil the thieves? The answer may lie in the fact that both houses, in Nice and in London, nestle close to their respective churches, encouraging, as I believe, the better operation of psychic forces.

Another experience also occurred near a church. My wife and I had accepted an invitation from an old friend to a party he was giving in his newly acquired country house in Gloucestershire. It was for a Saturday evening. Usually I excuse myself from any social engagement on Saturdays, especially if it may entail a late night, since this is likely to affect my concentration on Sunday services.

However, it was an unusual party with a mock battle as part of the entertainment. It was to commemorate a skirmish between Cavaliers and Roundheads which had taken place in the vicinity during the Civil War. Much intrigued by this and not having seen our host for nearly two years, I felt an exception could be made. Accordingly I arranged for my Sunday services to be conducted by a neighbouring priest, while we spent the weekend in Gloucestershire. As our friend already had a houseful of young guests, he arranged for us and a number of his other London friends to stay overnight at a charming hotel in a village about fifteen miles away.

It was a long drive from Hampstead and we arrived at the hotel barely an hour before the party was to begin. It was necessary to change into our evening clothes without delay. Being in such haste, we took very little stock of our surroundings, not even looking out of the window of our hotel bedroom while dressing. Immediately we were ready we hastened back to the car and followed the convoy of the other guests making for the party.

When it was over around midnight we drove back to the hotel. After so much driving during the day, together with the excitement of the evening, I felt so tired when we reached our room that I was in bed as soon as possible. My wife, on the contrary, was quite wakeful and, after turning out the lights, went over to the window and for the first time looked out. 'Goodness,' she called out, 'you ought to see this place. It's quite lovely. Come and see. It looks like a great quadrangle. There are big arches and the windows are lighted. There seems a great air of activity. It's really beautiful.'

She remained staring out for some moments. Drowsily I replied that I was just too tired and would see it all in the morning. I did, however, think it rather odd that when we returned to the hotel it had been in almost complete darkness. Yet now, apparently, there was this illumination. I felt a peculiar urge to get up and see for myself but fatigue got the better of me.

In the morning I got up earlier than my wife and took my first look out the window. It was a glorious sunny morning. Before me in sparkling splendour was beautiful grassland gently curving as far as the eye could see. There was no quadrangle, no arches, indeed no noticeable building even in the far distance. When I told my wife she could scarcely believe it. Coming to the window herself she could only say: 'But I saw it all quite clearly last night.'

At first I wondered if she had seen some reflection of the hotel building. But this was most unlikely. The architecture of it certainly did not suggest arches or quadrangles, and as for lighted windows I knew that the hotel had been in almost total darkness when we returned from the party, and even our own light was extinguished when my wife had looked out. Yet I, too, had observed a peculiar illumination reflecting on my wife's face as she had gazed out of the window that night. It was then I recalled that strange compulsion to see for myself when she had asked me to do so. It had been so strong that despite my tiredness I had lain awake for some while mentally fighting it. Now I realised the psychic nature of this experience. Even as I did so my wife put it into words.

'I know I saw it,' she said, 'and I am going to ask the proprietor if there used to be a building there. I think it must have been a monastery that I saw last night.' When she told him he did not seem at all surprised as she described what she had seen and her guess as to what it was. 'Let me see,' he said, 'you are in Room 12. That overlooks the site of an old monastic building which once stood there. I have a seventeenth-century print which shows it. From the way you have described it, what you saw was that building.'

Once again it is significant to point out that the hotel where we were staying is adjacent to a lovely old parish church. We had not realized this on our arrival, but after breakfast that morning the proprietor pointed out his personal gateway which led to it only a few yards away. This fact lends further support to the belief that sacred buildings and sites generate an atmosphere which stimulates the psychic senses. My own continuing regret is that I did not respond to my wife's request that night to come to the window. Ever since, I have wondered whether I would have seen what she saw and, if so, what I would have made of it.

It is also, I believe, of some significance that both of

these incidents took place not only near a church but in the period of late Saturday to early Sunday. Is it so fanciful to conceive that at such a time spiritual forces would be converging and concentrating? It is written that 'the evening and the morning' constitute each day. For the Christian it is on the first such day, Saturday night and Sunday, that the things of the spirit have been especially remembered. Then it is that man has offered his soul to God for the divine blessing, and rededicated it to his Creator in the glory of worship.

12

ASKING FOR HELP

The same combination of proximity to a church and the period of late Saturday and early Sunday seems to have stimulated the psychic faculties of a sixteen-year-old French girl. Catherine had won a year's scholarship to the French Lycée in London and we had offered her a home in the vicarage for the course of it.

It was after she had been with us for a couple of months and had settled down happily that the incident occurred. Very late one Saturday night she woke us by tapping nervously on our bedroom door and saying: 'Oh! *please* come.' She was in a great state of agitation and very white-faced.

'Whatever is the matter?' we asked.

'I keep seeing a person in my room', she said.

'How do you mean? What kind of person?'

'It is a man. He has staring eyes and he is very unhappy. He keeps asking me to help him. *Il est un fantôme.*'

'I will come', I said. 'Do not be afraid, Catie. Never be afraid of an apparition or ghost. It cannot hurt you. This one will go when I have said some prayers.'

Her room was on a floor above. Even as I went up the stairs I began to sense an oddness. On entering her room I was immediately struck by the uncanny chill in it. I distinctly felt a presence which made the hair on the nape of my neck bristle and caused a shiver down my spine. For one moment by the bedroom door and then at the foot of the girl's bed I became even more strongly aware of this brooding quality of unease. I could guess now what the girl meant. Catherine, who had followed me, was standing at the doorway still visibly shaken and wide-eyed. I told her to go downstairs and stay with my wife.

When she had left me I stood in the centre of the room. It took a few seconds before I felt really composed. Several times I felt compelled to turn about or look suddenly behind me. Once I even thought I was touched on the shoulder as if someone wished to draw my attention. It is very necessary to become tranquil oneself before dealing with an unhappy entity. Extending my hand as if in welcome I said: 'We understand you are disturbed. I will try to help you. Remember only and always his great love for you.' I kept silence for a space, meditating upon the compassion of Jesus for those who are troubled of heart.

The strange coldness departed almost instantly after that. Then I repeated the Lord's Prayer slowly, giving special thought to the phrase 'deliver us from evil'. The chill had given place to what can only be described as a glowing warmth. I felt confident that the unhappy presence had departed, and I returned to Catherine and my wife.

'Everything is all right now, my dear', I assured her. 'You will find your room quite peaceful and happy again. But, tell me, have you felt anything like this before?'

She nodded. 'Yes, I did not wish to tell you because you might think I was foolish. The same thing happened on several other Saturday nights recently. The man comes and always he is asking for help. He looks strange. His eyes stare. And he seems very sad.'

'Do you, then, see him so clearly?' I asked.

'I have been able to draw his face', she said. 'I will show you.'

She returned to her bedroom and came back to us carrying several sheets of squared paper from an exercise book. They were filled with the drawings of a man's head. He was bearded with wild staring eyes. Catherine had obviously made a number of attempts to capture his likeness as exactly as she could. All the drawings were basically alike. She had also made a number of notes. In these the same phrases were repeated with only slight variations: 'I NEED HELP. PLEASE WILL YOU HELP ME? I AM ALONE. GOD HAS LEFT ME.'

I asked her how she had felt when she had made her notes and sketches. From her attempts at explanations it was clear that she must have been in a semi-trance condition presumably because she had not fully awakened from her sleep. She felt her hand was being guided to make her drawings. The voice came to her at first in a whisper and then increased in volume and intensity. She would be awakened from a sound sleep to sense that someone was trying to capture her complete attention. Then she would see the apparition at the foot of her bed and it would begin its pleading.

On each occasion she found some relief by making her drawings and recording her messages. I began to think that the entity was desperately trying to establish its identity, but that was as much as I could make of the matter. We thought little more of the incident because Catherine was not troubled again after that night. We felt in any case it was best not to mention the subject unless she herself brought it up, but I kept in my desk the notes she had made.

Then something happened just two weeks later which threw light upon the matter. At any rate I am convinced it did. Catherine had gone home for the Easter holidays. A few days after she had left for Nice my wife and I were returning home from an evening engagement. As we were driving up to the vicarage we noticed a man passing the house. He paused and looked up at the windows. At first we were suspicious, for though we could not see him clearly there was something extremely odd about him. We even thought him rather sinister. It looked as if he were keeping a watch on the house. But he walked on in an absent sort of way. While we were putting the car in the garage, however, he looked back and saw us. Immediately he retraced his steps and asked if he could talk to me. I invited him into my study and when we were seated I took stock of him. He had a rather pale complexion, a short pointed black beard, and eyes which had a rather vacant stare about them.

His story was that he had for long been sure there was

66

some dark secret concerning his true parentage. His mother had recently died and he had unearthed some information which confirmed his suspicion that there was a skeleton in the family cupboard. I could not gather exactly what this information was though I did question him on it. He seemed vague rather than evasive about it. In fact after a few minutes of listening to him I came to the conclusion that he was suffering from some mental disturbance. His general facial expression, particularly his large staring eyes, together with his often uncompleted sentences which made it difficult to understand a good deal of his conversation, confirmed my opinion.

How could I help him? Why had he come to me? His eyes stared back at me almost apprehensively. 'I came', he said, 'because we both have the same surname. It is fairly unusual. I believe we are related. Therefore you could know what it was that happened about me.'

I could think of no dark secret to satisfy him. I mentioned the names of uncles and other relatives to see if they meant anything to him. Obviously they did not and, clearly, if there were any relationship between us it must have been very remote indeed. He was living some miles out of London and I wondered how he had found me. 'I have been to others who have the same name who are listed in various directories', he said. Apparently those he had called on had given him very short shrift. In most cases he had not been allowed to cross the threshold or explain his mission.

From his strange appearance I could well understand such reluctance. Although fairly tidy he did give the impression of one who might be begging. Indeed at first sight I had quite expected he would be asking me for money — not an uncommon object of quite a number who ring the vicarage doorbell. But it was not so. He had not come for a soft touch and money never entered our conversation even indirectly. Obviously he was genuine in his quest even if probably deluded about it.

67

Though I could not give him any real answer to his problem I tried to offer him what comfort and reassurance I could. In the light of the kind of reception he had received elsewhere I thought it would relieve his very evident apprehension if my wife gave him some coffee. It was very clear that such consideration affected him greatly for he now expatiated at some length on the unkindness and abruptness which he obviously felt he had met with in his other calls.

Apparently this had deterred him from making further inquiries for some months. However, noticing my name in a London directory, he finally summoned the courage to contact me. Even so he had thought deeply for several weeks before making his call that night. He had thought of telephoning me on more than one occasion but had always hesitated out of timidity. He had had to force himself to make this day's journey. During his conversation, which was practically a monologue for he scarcely allowed me to speak once, since he was convinced I could not enlighten him about his family, he would repeat that he felt so lost that he could see no purpose in living. Frustration would be his lot forever. Even God had abandoned him.

In this state of despair he now looked at me in such a strange way that quite suddenly something in me clicked in recognition. Surely this was the desperate, pleading expression which Catherine had described as that of the '*fantôme*' which had visited her? Moreover, the drawings she had made of the man's face were an amazing likeness of this unhappy fellow before me. She had spoken too of the particular pallor of the face as well as of the black pointed beard and large staring eyes. It was then that I knew what I must do to help him.

When he had lapsed at last into complete silence I said: 'I believe it is most likely that your birth is quite legitimate and that there is nothing terrible in your family background which can affect your life. Have no fear within yourself about this from now on. One thing I must tell you. God

68

never abandons us. Often we abandon him. It's never the other way round. You can come and see me again if ever you wish. If you want to telephone I shall listen. Don't be afraid that I will rebuff you. I shall never do that. There is one thing though that I can do now to help you. It is to pray for you.'

His eyes still stared at me but now some of the hopelessness had gone from them. When I rose from my chair and stood beside him I saw him close his eyes. It almost seemed as if he expected what followed. I put my hands on his head. 'Dear God,' I prayed aloud, 'you know this child of yours is deeply troubled. Sadness fills him so much that he cannot know the great and everlasting love you have for him. People have hurt him by their misunderstanding and impatience. Help him to realize they were not really aware of his great problem. So may he forgive them for their refusal to listen to him with courtesy. Now, dear Father, in your tender love give your peace to him. Set him free from the agony and doubt that fill him, for you are the God who cares and loves and forgives forever. In the name of the Father and of the Son and of the Holy Spirit may your soul be truly cleansed.'

At these last words he shook all over quite violently. In the last convulsion I felt something cold momentarily brush my forehead. This I took to be the departure of the demon causing his disorder since the shaking ceased altogether and he gently relaxed back into the chair, no longer stiffly leaning forward with nervousness and apprehension.

'Thank you, Father, for your healing love tonight', I concluded, and removed my hands gently. The room seemed very quiet and charged with a sweet tranquillity. When my visitor opened his eyes again the glazed stare had completely vanished. He looked normal and for the first time he smiled. 'Thank you for that', he said. 'I feel really better, as if a load has gone from me.'

'When you get home tonight,' I replied, 'don't think about your problem. You have thought about it very much at night, haven't you?' He nodded gravely. 'Particularly at weekends', he said. My mind reflected on the fact that Catherine's strongest psychic impression had occurred at a weekend. I continued: 'Nothing matters now but the way in which you live your life. It must be without fear. It must be without concern about something which may never have been and which, in any case, you were not responsible for. Remember you can see me again if you wish. God be with you.'

We shook hands and said good-night to each other. I watched him go down the street. He no longer walked in the furtive manner of his arrival. For a moment he looked back and saw that I was still watching him. He smiled, and this time it was more natural, like the leave-taking of an old friend. He raised his arm in farewell and then passed out of sight. I was not to hear from him again, and when Catherine returned to us after her Easter holiday she had no more visitations.

There is a further interesting point, however. Two years later my wife and I were again in Nice. Calling on Catherine's family, we felt we could now refer to the subject without distressing her. We were able to tell her of the man's visit to us of which she now heard for the first time. She was not over-surprised by our account, remarking that it was not the first time that people who were spiritually disturbed had appeared to her. Ruefully smiling, she said she seemed to attract them.

Catherine is a highly intelligent and gifted girl, very sensitive and deeply compassionate of all who suffer, perhaps to a degree unusual in one so young. She also said that when she was quite a child she had had a number of experiences, possibly highly vivid dreams, in which she had encountered unhappy souls who were pleading for her help. It is significant that her way home was always through the area of Holy Trinity, Nice and its churchyard, famous for the grave of Francis Lyte, author of the hymn 'Abide with Me'. In fact her bedroom overlooked this churchyard.

I am convinced that some departed souls who are deeply troubled attempt to communicate their anguish to us. Likewise I am sure that some very lonely and desperate souls in this life seek understanding and succour from their fellows through the activity of their spirit-souls, although unconsciously. This is because deep and prolonged absorption in a personal worry by someone who, for psychological or other reasons, is unable to obtain the required comfort and help through normal human contact is liable to produce a condition in which the desires and awareness of the body are virtually suspended, perhaps deliberately neglected.

Such an overwrought state can therefore induce trance. The soul then begins to act as pure spirit and will manifest, on an abnormal level, the properties of pure spirit. It will communicate directly with another soul if the latter is sufficiently receptive and is willing to have knowledge of it. The man who called on me during Catherine's Easter holiday may well have projected his distraught spirit-soul into her bedroom on those occasions of his deepest agony.

He had told me that the weekends were the periods in which he endured the highest pitch of mental frustration in seeking a sympathetic hearing. And it was at these times that Catherine received her perceptions of his 'phantom' presence. He may not have been deliberately engineering it, but when a person is in a highly emotional or mentally disordered state such a projection is likely. Catherine's very sensitive and compassionate nature would, I believe, have made her a natural target for an unhappy soul which was hoping to derive from the vicarage the comfort and long-sought answer it needed. Once it had found her to be a willing listener it would continue to visit her for relief. It follows that the encouragement of her sympathy would have heartened the spirit-soul of the man so much that he finally found the courage he needed to make his call on me.

13

DISTURBED IN THE NIGHT

I experienced on another occasion this ability of a profoundly disturbed soul to appear in a dream. At one time a newcomer to my congregation was a young accountant. He had recently left college and worked for a well-known firm. He showed great interest in parish affairs and when he seemed keen to do youth work I was glad of his assistance. It was soon evident that he was not only helpful but popular and effective.

Then I began to have a bout of restless nights, very unusual for me as I am normally a sound sleeper. Each time I woke I found my mind was dwelling upon this young man. There was something which caused me great agitation though I could not make out what it was. On the last occasion my concern became so oppressive that I lay awake for several hours quite unable to rid myself of a presentiment that something was seriously wrong. I tried desperately to sort it all out but remained nonplussed and confused. It just did not make sense. Finally, utterly exhausted, I fell asleep.

The very next evening I had a visit from the young man's girl-friend. She seemed very agitated and I asked her into my study, where she immediately began to explain that she was very worried about him. She hastened to add that though there had been a deep bond between them she could not contemplate marriage to him. It was sympathy she had for him, not love.

'Why sympathy?' I asked.

'Because he leans on me', she replied. 'He cannot cope unless he is able to see me every now and then. I have tried to break things off but he becomes so distressed that I fear for him.'

'Fear for him?' I queried. 'That's a bit strong, isn't it?'

'Oh, no,' she answered, 'you see I was at university with him. His home was an unhappy one, and when I met him one day at a lecture he confided in me. I tried to cheer him up and give him confidence, but it all got so deep. Not that I really wanted it that way. In the end he used to say that without my interest he would take his life.'

'Sometimes young men say such things', I said. 'It adds drama to their romantic life. It is not to be taken all that seriously.'

'But it wasn't like that', she hastily broke in. 'He really did mean it. I know it. Sometimes he would be so depressed that it was quite awful to see him, and to hear him. He would say he would be unable to continue with his studies if I left him. It worried me so much — that last year before the finals.'

'Did he believe that you cared for him — more than just friendship, I mean?' I asked her.

'Yes, he did. Mind you, I did like him. I was not just sorry for him. In some ways he was like a child. I think he still is. I felt protective towards him, I think. But I tried hard not to encourage him to believe there could ever be more than friendship between us. He needed help and I couldn't refuse it. He was so much alone at college. Except for me he seemed to have no one. And certainly his family were hopeless.'

'Well, what do you think I can do?' I asked.

'I feel he must at last face up to the fact that we can't go on seeing each other. Perhaps you could persuade him. In the last week or so the situation has become absolutely frantic. He calls on me late at night and disturbs the other tenants. He even tried to climb through my window on one occasion. Sometimes I feel I must call the police.'

'That's a bit drastic,' I said, 'though I must say he seems to go too far. Is it absolutely impossible for you to reason with him?'

She looked at me for a few moments. 'I can see', she

answered at last, 'that you don't know everything. I thought perhaps you did — that maybe he had told you himself.'

I must have looked nonplussed. 'Know what?' I asked. 'He seems a very nice fellow to me.'

'You didn't know he takes drugs?' she queried. 'That there are times when he is quite beside himself?'

I must have shown my surprise at this revelation. 'Why no, I did not. I have never suspected anything like that. He always seemed on the ball to me.'

'Maybe,' she said, 'but I can tell you that now it's got pretty bad. You haven't seen him for two weeks or so, have you?'

'True', I replied. 'But as the youth club is not meeting for a month I am not unduly surprised at not seeing him.'

'It all started at college in his last year', she continued. 'I did try to help him and that's when he began to depend on me to get him through. Sometimes I wondered if he would ever make his degree. In the end I don't think he ever went home during the vacations. He would try to spend most of them at my home.'

'Has he had any medical help?' I inquired. 'About the drugs, I mean?'

'No, and I think he is at the stage when he badly needs a doctor. He came to my place again last night and he was in such a state I phoned for an ambulance. But he went off before it arrived.'

At about this point in the conversation the doorbell rang and I left her to see who was calling. To my surprise the young man himself stumbled through the door even before I could invite him in. He was obviously upset and appeared to have been crying. 'I must see you', he said. 'Please can I talk to you?' Even as he spoke he was ahead of me and into my study. His girl-friend looked taken aback at first, but when he suddenly rushed towards her and buried his head in her lap she was evidently deeply touched by his condition. When I saw that she was caressing his head and talking quietly to him in an effort to comfort him I thought

I would leave them alone for a while. When I returned he seemed calmer and was seated in an easy chair beside her. She rose as if to leave. 'He wants to talk to you now', she said. 'Don't go yet,' I replied, 'my wife has just made coffee. Won't you stay for a cup with her?'

I took her to the drawing-room where my wife immediately tried to set her at ease. When I returned to my study the young man was sitting with his head buried in his hands. He looked utterly dejected. When I spoke to him I found that after his first few sentences he was incoherent. I thought it best not to interrupt him with questions until he had gained more control of himself. But then it suddenly happened. He began to writhe and twist and grimace most alarmingly. For a few seconds it did not dawn on me that I was seeing the spasms of drug-taking. The convulsions became so horrifying that I thought he would collapse any moment. In his babblings I could see he was trying to ask me not to leave him.

I felt I should telephone a doctor or at least summon his girl-friend back to the study. Something, however, restrained me from doing either. It was not only the sense I had caught of his pleading for me not to leave him even for a moment. There was something more, a gathering realization that this was profound spiritual torment, not the shocking symptons of drugs alone. I recalled my recent nocturnal misgivings and especially the oppressive feeling which had so troubled me during the previous night.

An inner voice seemed to speak to me. It was reassuring and stilled the agitation which the sight of the young man had aroused in me. I thought that the voice was saying: 'Reach out to his spirit-soul. Work at that level, and trust wholly in the Father.'

I gently released his hands which were clutching the sleeves of my jacket. Then, standing behind his chair, I placed my hands on his head. Suddenly a vivid picture of Christ came to me without effort — almost without any meditative preparation. Silently I said: 'Come, Lord Jesus, to us now and give your healing and peace to this thy child.' Aloud I said: 'In the name of Jesus Christ I command this evil to depart from you.'

For a few moments I was aware that there was a cold-ness being transmitted to my hands. I have sensed the same when I have sought healing for hospital patients who have recently been given drugs to ease pain or to induce relaxa-tion. At first there is this coldness, a kind of negative feel-ing. It persists for a while, but if prayer is maintained it usually gives way to the positive sense of tingling warmth.

The convulsions eased to a little tremor and the young man began to speak intelligently again. 'I am so sorry about this, Vicar', he said. 'Forgive me. I wanted so much to come and see you last night but it was so late in the end that I felt I couldn't. So I made a fool of myself and went to see Betty. It was absolutely mad, but I felt I must see somebody. I imagine she came here tonight to tell you?'

I nodded. 'Yes, but not only that. Betty is deeply con-cerned about you. As for seeing me, of course you can do that however late. My job wouldn't make much sense if I couldn't see people when they were most desperate, would it? And you can always pick up the phone.'

As he was now fully himself I urged him to face up to the fact that this girl-friend was genuine in her attitude that she could not be more than a friend to him. 'I realize that,' he said, 'deep down I do. But it is so hard to stop loving. I certainly don't want to upset her again like last night.' A little later we joined my wife and Betty for coffee and I hoped that matters would be happily resolved. He was to move away from the district shortly afterwards and eventually took up another post, which was probably the best thing.

I recount this incident only because it suggests, I think, further proof that when a person is very emotionally dis-turbed or has taken drugs the spirit-soul may be partially released. It will then act almost as pure spirit. Able, that is, to overcome the barrier of space and the limitations of the body and so communicate directly with another person.

This young man, in the extreme stress produced by the combination of deep emotional turmoil and the effect of drugs, was fervently desiring to unburden his sense of guilt to me by making a clean breast of everything. His pride had been holding him back from doing this for some time. I had shown trust and high regard for his qualities. What would I think of him now if I knew of his uncommendable behaviour towards his girl friend and the secret of his drug-taking? At last the mental agony was such that his spirit-soul desired above all else to inform my own of his intolerable burden. Hence this attempted communication with me in the night watches which had so disturbed and oppressed me.

14

THE PRESENCE OF EVIL

In ancient times belief in demon-possession was prevalent. Life's adversities and man's physical and mental maladies, especially the latter, were thought to be caused by evil spirits which had gained a hold over the unfortunate person. Today we are more enlightened. Medical science long ago discarded such ideas and has advanced rapidly for that very reason. Nevertheless I am convinced that we cannot reject altogether the possibility that evil entities could be the cause of some illnesses. I believe that evil does exist in demonic form which sometimes attaches itself to the human personality. It is difficult to prove this but certain psychic experiences have made me doubt whether sickness is always an entirely impersonal affliction.

If human beings are possible subjects for demon-possession, then there must be a case for the practice of exorcism. Exorcism is the act of expelling evil spirits from persons and places. The history of most parts of the world bears record of this practice and its special ceremonies. Much of this is pure superstition and must be dismissed as mumbo-jumbo of the most primitive and barbaric kind. None the less I believe there is a kernel of truth buried within this outer husk of dark trappings and ignorance.

In the case I now relate I am certain an evil entity was active. I was asked to see a young woman who had gone into hospital for an operation on her eyes. It was feared that she would become completely blind. She was very devout and when I called at the hospital she specially asked for the laying-on of hands. After praying with her I laid my hands on her head. There was an immediate vibration in them which went right through my body. Afterwards she said it was like receiving an electric shock which suddenly illuminated the region behind her eyes with a brilliant flash of light. I had actually quoted the words of Jesus to her during my prayer for healing: 'I am the Light of the world.' She always maintained that the small portion of sight still preserved to her was due to that moment. She was quite sure that otherwise she would have been totally blind. Apparently she sensed that a measure of healing had been given in that hour.

I discovered later that she had had several mental breakdowns, and the day was to come when I was to witness one. She telephoned early one morning and talked at great speed, without pausing more than a few seconds for any answer to the various questions she asked me. Sometimes her voice was quiet and even but then it would rise and become excitable, sometimes tearful. As she continued I became more and more alarmed and in the end realized I must go to her for fear she come to any harm. I went straight to her house and found her in a highly emotional state. While she got ready to return home with me, because I felt my wife and I could look after her there, I was alone in her living room. It felt very peculiar and psychically disordered. Something like a small altar had been erected on the mantelpiece. There was a cross, two candles on either side which had obviously been burning for a considerable time, and some flowers in tiny vases. Various objects, some as I discovered later of great sentimental importance, were heaped together on a table. Others, which she told me she had taken a special dislike to mainly because of their association with her childhood, she had put outside the front door.

When we reached home she sat in my study. In the kitchen I whispered to my wife that perhaps we should telephone the girl's doctor. To my astonishment, when I returned to the study, which was a considerable distance away and with two closed doors between, she declared that she had overheard me and that I must not send for him. In any case, she said, she would be seeing him that same evening. My wife gave her some tea, which seemed to calm her a little. At lunch-time she was still very distraught, rambling on about her unhappy childhood and her mother's lack of affection. I thought that much of what she said was due to the state she was in. There was very little opportunity for me to counsel her in any way, as she rarely paused long enough in her monlogue to let me finish what I was saying even when she did put a direct question to me.

When lunch ended she became very quiet for a time. Then, looking fixedly ahead, she suddenly asked me if I liked the poetry of Rupert Brooke. Before I could reply she said there was a copy of his poems on my bookshelf. This statement astonished me because her back was towards the shelves and she had not once looked at them since she came in. She had been much too preoccupied with her troubles, and in any case her sight was too poor to single out this slim volume of poetry amongst all the hundreds of other books.

'That's true', I said. 'I have got a copy. It's somewhere behind you. Would you like it? I'll try and find it for you.' I got up to go to the shelves. Without turning her head she said: 'It's in the far end block of books in the third shelf from the top.' 'Goodness, you are right', I said. 'I had forgotten exactly where it was myself. But how did you know? And how did you know I had a volume anyway?'

I began to think that she must be in a trance and in this condition her spirit-soul was obtaining the necessary knowledge about my library. She did not answer but, still staring fixedly ahead, she began to recite Rupert Brooke's poem, 'The Soldier'. Clearly, most beautifully, and without hesitation, she quoted it right through. It was uncanny. Uncanny because after talking excitedly and often irrationally from seven o'clock in the morning almost without a break till after one o'clock in the afternoon, she could calmly recite this lovely poem. It seemed that in the very words, with their cadence and rhythm, she was finding a way of release.

When she had finished my wife and I spontaneously

congratulated her. She told us that English had been her favourite subject at school and that she had won many prizes for verse-speaking and drama. As she spoke it seemed to us that she thought she was back at school and that her teacher was applauding and encouraging her efforts.

By now I could see she had exhausted all her nervous energy and was beginning to relax. I hoped that the storm had passed. She had constantly emphasized during her almost unceasing flow of words that she felt she was in the grip of evil. The atmosphere in the room was certainly very strange. There was a sense of horror and repulsion, a kind of barrier surrounding her which was icy cold. It made me recoil when I went towards her. In fact I found it so disconcerting that I drew back a step. Then I stood quite still about five feet from her and prayed, silently at first. I centred my mind on the thought of Christ's exorcism of the demoniac who dwelt in the tombs of the country of the Gerasenes.

I allowed these mental pictures to come vividly alive in my imagination. Then, very suddenly, I felt an intake of power as if my whole being were coming under its control. My breathing quickened and my chest heaved as if it were imprisoning a force that must come gushing out or I would burst. As if in a dream I stepped to her side. She was muttering inaudibly but, as I raised my hands in the air above her, she cried out, 'Take it from me! Please take it from me!'

That barrier of cold which emanated from her appeared to press around me. Then I felt as if my body were dissolving and something deep within it being liberated. The command which came from me at last was uttered under a powerful compulsion, and seemed to be the climax of a great struggle which had taken place inside me. 'In the name of Jesus Christ, come out of her!' Then I described a circle about her with my hands, at the same time saying: 'Surround her, dear Lord, with the circle of thy divine protection.'

Immediately after pronouncing these words I experienced the most awesome sensation. It swept over me like the wash of an ice-cold wave. Uncontrollable shudders went down my spine and the hair on the back of my head seemed to rise. The chill was so intense that even on that warm summer's day I shivered. I remembered the words of St James, in his Epistle to the Church in Jerusalem: 'The demons also believe [there is one God] and tremble.'

It was as if some evil and horrifying thing were trying to seize me. The room itself was filled with its malevolent presence. To describe such experiences exactly is impossible. The best I can do is to say that I felt that something evil, which was completely other than this woman and myself, was battling for the mastery over us. I am convinced that a power so concentrated as to appear tangible must have been a demon which had gained a hold over her and had to be exorcised.

Unhappily I cannot say that she was cured from that moment. I believe that the demon was not fully exorcised by my ministration. It is well recorded that exorcism is not always completed on the first occasion but that a repetition of it may be necessary, even several times, to ensure the final eviction of the malevolent spirit or spirits. I have often wondered whether prolonged effort would eventually have proved successful. However, this was not possible partly because soon afterwards she moved too far away to make this practicable but mainly because she went into hospital, and I make it a rule not to conduct exorcism if psychiatric treatment is being given. Certainly long years of such treatment have not cured her.

A number of clergy believe that some mental illness may be due to demon-possession and there is evidence to support their view. The Roman Catholic Church has indeed a special rite of exorcism. I can do no more than place on record those peculiar reactions which suggested that a chilling and repugnant power was present and that this alien force provided definite physical sensations of coldness and blustering energy when commanded to come forth in the name of Jesus Christ.

15

A FEARFUL EXORCISM

One of the most disturbing experiences I have known suggests the possibility of demonic influence upon innocent people living in a place where black arts have been practised. Two sisters, both attractive young business girls, had taken a flat together. One of them was a regular churchgoer and it was she who telephoned me one morning, obviously very upset, to say that she and her sister were suffering terribly from what she described as a fearful haunting. This had gone on for many nights since they had taken over the flat so that neither of them was able to sleep peacefully, with the result that they were now almost desperate with exhaustion.

'You must think us crazy, Vicar,' the girl said, 'but it is absolutely true. We are just terrified of another night here without something being done.' 'I know how level-headed you are', I replied. 'If you say there is something pretty foul in your flat which is depriving you and your sister of sleep then something must be done about it very quickly. These things may be rare but they do happen and they can be really dreadful sometimes. Come and see me tonight and tell me the full story.'

Had I not known her to be an intelligent girl with an extremely responsible job I would have found the story she had to tell very hard to believe. She and her sister shared a bedroom with separate beds. Soon after they had fallen asleep her sister would wake up in terror saying that someone was trying to drag her to the window as if intending to throw her out of it. The sensation was so frightening that they decided to keep this window firmly fastened despite the fact that it was a hot August. When she was woken by her sister's screams she would see a large shape hovering over her sister's bed. It would remain for some seconds while both girls lay so frozen with horror that they could not move. Apparently the atmosphere of the room would become so powerfully charged with evil and dread that for the rest of the night neither of them would be able to sleep.

When she had finished her story she asked if my wife and I would come to the flat that same evening. 'Maybe you would say some prayers, or do whatever you think will expel this evil presence, which I am sure is intending to do us great harm.'

We decided to go with her immediately, and I put on my cassock and took with me a small wooden cross. I had never been to their flat before but as I turned my car into the road I thought that, if I had been asked to select any particular house to serve as a film set for a haunted mansion, this particular one could certainly have been it. It was a very warm evening in the late summer and already dusk, but that house must have had a dark and forbidding appearance even in full sunshine. In that light it looked utterly grim.

We followed the girl up the sombre stone steps to the front door along a gloomy passage and up the first flight of stairs. This opened on to a landing. When we reached it I became quite suddenly aware of a definite drop in temperature. I called out to the others who were ahead of me and already going up the next staircase. 'Wait a moment', I said. 'Surely there is something strange right here. This feels like a trouble spot.' I paused outside a door.

'You feel it too?' asked the girl. 'Is there a lavatory behind this door?' I asked. 'It is so odd. Did someone hang himself in there?' She nodded. 'I understand someone committed suicide there, or tried to. I am not sure which. No one here now was a tenant at the time, but I heard a rumour when we first came. We have certainly felt something strange there at times. But come up here and see what you think.'

We went into the flat, which had been made by closing off the upper part of this large Victorian house. The sister was there and most grateful to see us. I explained I would go to each corner of their large bed-sitting room and try to sense if there were anything peculiar. Would they, therefore, keep as quiet as possible to help my concentration?

Within a few seconds of standing still in the middle of the room I felt an even stronger repetition of the kind of sensation I had experienced on the landing below. I went over to a corner of the room and there the fall of temperature was even more marked. I felt my skin prickle all over. The icy chill began to gather a kind of force within it and the hair on my head seemed to rise from my scalp. It was a most unpleasant sensation. Almost without thinking I found myself saying: 'In the name of the Father and of the Son and of the Holy Spirit, begone.'

Still holding the little cross before me I moved to the next two corners. There the sensations were less acute, but on reaching the last corner I experienced the most violent reaction. It caused me to shake from head to foot. It was so awful that I could scarcely move my lips to pronounce the exorcising prayer.

Then I noticed that I was standing before a low cupboard built into the wall. 'There's something evil in there', I said. 'What is inside?' They explained that it contained a suit-case left behind by the former tenant, an African, and they were hoping that he or a friend might soon call back for it. 'You must not keep it here', I said. 'Leave it in the hall of the house if you like, but get rid of it from this place. I think the cupboard, and possibly this empty case, contained something unpleasant — perhaps associated with magic or devil worship.'

I remained silent for a minute or two in that particular corner. All the while the coldness continued. I was about to say a prayer aloud when I suddenly felt a presence in front of me so repellent that it was like receiving a blow. In fact I thought it would throw me to the floor. It was like the unexpected shock one receives when almost colliding with a substantial object in a dark building, drawing back just in time to save oneself from injury. In this case, however, there was not only the sense of a barrier being suddenly erected but of a violent malevolence which was personally intent on overcoming me so that my prayers would not be made. The next sensation was even more horrifying, for I felt that my clothes and even my flesh were being stripped from me. My tongue began to cleave to the roof of my mouth so that I could not speak. Every limb became rigid and I thought my heart had ceased to beat. I have never known such indescribable apprehension.

Darkness was closing in all around me and I was becoming as one petrified. Just as I felt my mind was on the brink of complete eclipse I realized that only the power of Christ could deal with this vindictive and horrific entity and what it was trying to do to me. That realization broke the spell and I experienced an inflow of wholesome power which came like a cool, fresh breeze to raise me up. In that moment my tongue was loosened. 'Lord Jesus,' I prayed aloud, 'drive far from this place the snares of evil and may thy holy angels dwell here to preserve us in peace.'

Then I asked the others to say the Lord's prayer with me. After this I felt the atmosphere was much better. Before my wife and I went home I left the little cross with the sisters, as they said it would be a comfort to them. But as I went down the front steps of that house I felt I was being pursued by a strange and most evil spirit. Driving back home I felt just as if the awful thing I had aroused in the flat were still right behind me. It was all I could do not to take my eyes from the road ahead and look over my shoulder. I felt that it must be bent on my destruction. In fact on several occasions during that journey I asked my wife if she would turn round and see if there were someone at my back in the rear seat of the car. The sense of pursuit was terribly strong and real.

But there was much worse to come. For the rest of the

evening I could not shake off this feeling of being followed wherever I went. Constantly I looked over my shoulder, even swivelling abruptly about, thinking that I might catch a sight of whatever it was. Finally we went to bed but I continued to be uneasy and, I must admit, frightened. I could not bear the bedside lamp to be switched off and for a long time we kept it on. Every now and then my whole body would be shaken with uncontrollable tremors and my spine feel icy cold. Over and over again I tried to describe to my wife the awful horror I was enduring. Later she was to tell me that my face had gone white as chalk, my cheeks were hollow and my eyes staring ahead as if I had had a terrible shock or seen some ghastly sight.

All the time I felt I was desperately fighting an alien force which was seeking to master me. I tried to find relief through reading my bedside Bible but could not concentrate for more than a few verses. The best I could do was to think of Jesus, and I found particular comfort in the scene of him teaching the disciples his special prayer. But even so the alarm would return and I would shake violently from head to foot and again the sense of dread would engulf me. Eventually, exhausted, I must have dropped off to sleep for about half an hour, only to awaken quite suddenly, gasping for breath. I felt as if two strong hands were firmly and inexorably dragging my head from my shoulders. I was absolutely powerless to move.

This was worse than any nightmare, for I knew I was fully awake and felt that I was fighting for my very life. My whole body had gone quite rigid and those seeming hands at my throat were choking me. It was the most shocking experience, and even as I now write about it the lingering memory of its vile horror makes me hesitate. On the very few occasions I have recounted this matter I relive something of the terror of it and I shudder, if ever so slightly, in the recalling.

Suddenly, the paralysis in my throat was broken and I cried out with a loud voice, invoking the help of Almighty

God. Then I saw a dark shape flit across the room at the foot of the bed and go towards the open window through which brilliant moonlight was shining. The curtains were undrawn and the room was quite light. My wife, who was already a-wake, sensed also the horror of the atmosphere, and then something made both of us look towards our bedroom windows. Neither of us dared to mention the fact at the time but afterwards we admitted to having seen a strange wizened face, like that of a shrunken head, hovering at the top of the open window. It remained for several seconds staring at us and the evil generated from it filled the room. Then it disappeared abruptly.

This affair made me realize how important it is that our prayers for God's protection against the powers of evil should not be considered perfunctory or out of date but should be truly meant. Above all we must maintain our whole trust in the almightiness of our heavenly Father who eternally wills our good. I think it underlines also the great danger of dabbling in occult practices and particularly in efforts to contact the spirit world. We can lay ourselves open to malignant forces which may cause serious psychological disorder. Certainly all such experiments should be supported by strong belief in the lordship of Jesus Christ over the spiritual realm.

I know that the sense of evil haunted me for over a fortnight. I became so pale and drawn that a neighbour spoke of my shocked appearance. In the end I mentioned the matter to Canon Pearce-Higgins, then sub-dean of Southwark Cathedral, a friend for many years and President of the Churches' Fellowship of Psychical Study. He advised me to use the special prayer for divine protection to guard the soul from satanic forces and asked members of the Fellowship to include my situation in their prayers.

Using the special prayer gave temporary relief for maybe an hour or two at a time, and gradually the sense of evil pursuit began to lessen in intensity. I must say that one night my wife, determined that something drastic should be done to lay this evil spirit, swept through the house like a whirlwind with a broom! Little did she realize then that in this vigorous exercise she was doing precisely what the old manuals have prescribed for ridding a place of demons. The continued tradition of 'beating the bounds' is a relic of this ancient practice. At any rate her effort was also most effective in temporarily easing the haunting from me.

The final lifting of the malevolent influence came when I had been soaking in a hot bath for an hour. Several times I was conscious of this relentless entity during that time. The prolonged torment of it depressed me terribly. I was almost in despair thinking that normal life would never return. In one supreme effort to bring the forces of good to bear I called upon God to deliver me and then, with great earnestness and concentration, I stood up and described a circle about my body with my hands, my arms stretched fully at shoulder level, beginning in front and then moving them slowly and deliberately round until my finger-tips met behind me. At the same time I said aloud: 'Lord Jesus, in whom I completely trust, I know that thou hast power and authority over all the world of the spirit; deliver me now from every evil and surround me with the circle of thy divine protection.' The effect of this prayer was almost instantaneous. As I lay back again in the water I felt a surge of confidence and such exquisite peace that I hardly dared to breathe in case I dissipated it. It was a truly benevolent experience. The happiness and the sense of complete release it bestowed were so beautiful that my heart overflowed with thanksgiving. I think I wept with the sheer wonder and exhilaration of it. In that lovely cleansing I knew, without any lingering doubt, that the entity had been banished and I was exorcised.

The final act in the drama concerns the two sisters. Finding that the evil thing, whatever it was, still troubled them, though very much less than before, I said they should come into my church for the laying-on of hands. I thought it essential that this should be done in a holy place, for I felt that prayers offered in that strange house were only agitating, and not effectually relieving, the evil. The two girls came to church together and I gave them the laying-on of hands. I also described the circle of protection about them with the appropriate prayer. Immediately the temperature in the church seemed to fall sharply. My wife, who was also praying there with us, said afterwards that it felt as if something very cold had brushed her face.

A few minutes after the two girls had left the church a third and younger sister came in. She did not share their flat but had been worried about them. Unlike her sisters who had come solemnly and received great reassurance and peace, this girl arrived more or less lightheartedly. But the moment she received the laying-on of hands she trembled violently and her face went almost green. She had to rush outside to be sick. The physical change which came over her was sudden and complete and she was obviously very frightened, but after sipping a glass of water she returned to normal and was none the worse afterwards.

My own belief is that the entity, having been driven away from her two sisters in the earlier exorcism had tried to affect her and had likewise been discharged. The chill presence which my wife had noticed was, I believe, the entity seeking another human being to dwell in. My wife, who has a strong personality, and had already done battle with it, would have proved too inhospitable for it. I am convinced therefore that it sought a place in the young sister but was exorcised too promptly to gain any real hold.

However, the strangeness of the atmosphere in the church after all this had taken place so disturbed and concerned me that for several minutes I knelt at the altar and prayed, giving special thanks to God for the victorious power of Christ and the company of angels. Finally I prayed that any unquiet spirits might go in peace and leave the church as a true place of sanctity for the adoration of God the Father and of his Son. From that day on the sisters had no further haunting and the awful feeling of horror and pursuit ceased completely.

Churches can and should be centres of highly curative and powerful psychic forces which promote physical as well as spiritual well-being. This is testified enough by people who rarely wander into a church but, when they do, find at least in some an exceptional and very real sense of peace and comfort. They cannot explain it but obviously they feel this to be so in some deep fashion and will frankly remark on it. It is our prayers and the prayers of those in ages past and, we hope, of those yet to come which impregnate a church with God's blessings of peace, hope, and consolation. These are the continuing thirsts of every generation and certainly of every human soul at some time or other in his or her life.

The majority of people today may not consciously understand the meaning and relevance of churches. They probably hardly even notice them when they pass. But a house of God is none the less essential to hold back the invisible onslaught of evil forces which continually seek a hold upon the world in which men live. Every church community should strive to recognize this profound significance which it has amid what so often appears to be an unnoticing and cynical community. Its faithful members, however small their number, should be greatly fortified and encouraged by the conviction that they, through their constant worship and steadfastness in prayer, are protecting the whole community from what would otherwise be an unrestrained power of malevolent and destructive psychic force. They are virtually at work on God's business on behalf of all men, however pagan. Earlier ages put it more simply by seeing the church 'family' as the weapon which, in the all-conquering power of Christ, engaged a constant warfare against Satan.

The other fact shown up by this experience is the danger of ignorant dabbling in the occult, especially in the practice of spiritism. Most amateurs use a planchette or ouija board in order to obtain messages from the spirit world.

These experiments may often begin lightheartedly and amount to nothing. But sometimes an individual of nervous or highly strung temperament may be seriously affected during a seance and become open to damaging entities which seriously disturb normality and may even result in a mental breakdown.

The ouija board acts as the focus of concentration which induces trance and thus permits the powers of the spirit-soul to manifest. Unless the subject, who is now virtually in a hypnotic state, is very firmly convinced of the supremacy of the goodness and love of God, he or she may then succumb to the attack of malevolent spirits intent on invading a personality which has been laid wide open to them. I am particularly saddened by the number of young people who have been badly affected by indulging in such practices, often just to have a new sensation.

In some cases I have had to use exorcism to dispel these fears afterwards, or talked to them for hours in an effort to help them understand their predicament and so rescue them from it. I have described my own experience mainly to show the psychological disturbance that evil entities can cause in their attempt to separate us from the reality of our normal life. Should they succeed our minds could become totally unhinged, and we would then live in a twilight world. The realm of spirits is a dangerous one indeed to enter if unprotected by the armour of faith in the all-conquering goodness and love of God as declared to us in Jesus Christ.

16

AN EARLY MORNING EXORCISM

One morning we were woken by the ringing of our bedside telephone. A man's voice said: 'Would you come and do something about a haunting?' He sounded urgent and agitated, and said he had asked the local police station for our telephone number. As it was barely three o'clock in the morning the officer on duty had tried to dissuade him from telephoning, but my caller felt so shaken and worried by what was happening that he thought it important that I should come to his house while the atmosphere of the haunting still persisted.

The address he gave was not far away, and within a quarter of an hour I was there. It was a house with several tenants and there were a number of bell-pushes. I was trying to scan the names under them when a light shone in the hallway and a man in dark trousers and white singlet opened the front door and asked me to follow him. At the end of the passage a woman with a woollen dressing-gown over her night-dress was standing. The light was not good but I could see that she was sickly pale and looked extremely distressed.

The man introduced her to me as his wife and the two of them led me into their bedroom. At first sight I thought a cyclone must have torn through it. It was not a very large room and the disorder in it made it seem quite claustrophobic. The curtains were partially drawn but all askew and the bedclothes were in a state of complete disarray. By the one narrow window a small dressing-table was covered with a chaos of bits and pieces, some of which had evidently been knocked over and were scattered about the floor. I found the atmosphere of the room very oppressive and it made me uneasy. Almost immediately I said to the couple:

'The trouble is here, isn't it?' They both nodded.

'Tell me, what you have been experiencing?' I asked. The man did most of the talking: 'I am home on leave from the Army in Northern Ireland', he replied. 'I came back for my grandmother's funeral just over a week ago. She always looked after me because my mother died when I was small. My wife and I have not been married very long, about a year, and my grandmother never approved of our marriage, never liked my wife. Well, ever since the funeral our flat has felt awful. Every night we have felt my grandmother was here in this room. I wake up and feel I am being urged to hurt my wife. It frightens me. Tonight was the worst ever because my wife says I was trying to strangle her even while I was asleep. When I did wake up it's true my hands were round her throat. I'm scaring her terribly and now I'm afraid of what I might do without knowing it.'

'Have you seen much of the trouble in Northern Ireland?' I inquired. 'My God, yes', he answered. 'But if you think it may have affected me, given me nightmares or something, I can assure you that isn't so. You see my wife feels this thing, too — that my grandmother is here. She was a pretty strange woman, you know.' I looked at him. Tall, strong, clean-cut, a typical soldier. Hardly the kind of person, I thought, who would be over-imaginative or susceptible to cranky ideas.

'Do you find trouble in the day-time', I asked, 'in any other part of the flat?'

His wife said that she often felt that the grandmother was present when she was working in the kitchen. 'I feel sometimes that she is right behind me,' she explained, 'and when I do it upsets me so much that I get flustered and go cold all over.'

'Have you a photograph of her?' I asked.

'No, not here,' the man replied, 'but there is something of hers which we feel is wrong. I have her wedding ring, and somehow that unsettles both of us. I suppose I should not have kept it.'

'It gives me the creeps', his wife added.

I asked for some water in a small bowl and explained to them that I would bless the water and mark with it the sign of the cross on each door of their flat and pray for God's blessing on their home. I asked, also, that the three of us be silent for a while in order that we might recollect that we were in the presence of God. It was during this silence that a thought occurred to me. 'Can I have that ring for a moment?' I asked. The man fetched it from the mantelshelf. It was a very small, plain gold wedding-ring. Clearly his grandmother had had a tiny hand or very slender fingers. I had already asked her Christian name, which was Margaret.

'Would you say your grandmother was a religious woman?' I asked. He thought for a moment and then nodded: 'I would say so. Certainly at one time she went to church quite regularly. I know she taught me my prayers as a child. Yes, she was religious. More than most these days, anyway.'

We were silent again. This time I began to sense a rather disturbing presence. I had closed my eyes to aid concentration but opened them fleetingly and saw that the man and his wife were completely attentive to my suggestion of stillness. Their eyes were downcast and their hands were clasped in their laps in the attitude of prayer. I noted also that the man's face had become almost as pale as his wife's.

The uncomfortable feeling of a discordant presence in the place intensified and I felt a marked chill. I believe that these lowerings of temperature which accompany the manifestation of entities are due to the fact that they need to use physical energy in order to make their presence felt by us. This energy may be taken from our bodies and therefore we feel a temperature loss.

I prayed aloud: 'We know there is a troubled spirit here. If it is you, Margaret —'. At this mention of the Christian name I had to break off abruptly because I felt that my right hand, which was holding the ring, was being clamped tight as in a vice. The pressure built up and became so great that my fingernails dug painfully into my palm. I tried to

95

open my hand a little to relieve the pressure but could not do so. I realized now that I was involved in a spiritual contest. This ring was the vehicle of matter through which I was exercising the faculty of my spirit-soul.

I became more confident, feeling I was on the right track. 'Margaret,' I resumed, 'if it is you, why do you not go to that place of beauty and contentment which has been prepared for you by our heavenly Father? There is nothing here for you now. Only sadness and distress for others and yourself. In a moment I shall be blessing this home in the name of the Father and of the Son and of the Holy Spirit, and asking God's holy angels to preserve it in peace. You will know what that means.'

My hand remained fiercely clenched round the ring so that my knuckles had turned snow white. There were tremors all along my forearm. 'Margaret, the Lord Jesus in whom you trust and who is the lover of your soul desires to receive you, to go with you. Margaret, we are praying for you that you may leave joyfully in peace. We are now going to say the prayer of Jesus, and may you go to the happy abode he has prepared for you.'

I asked the man and his wife to join with me in saying the Lord's Prayer. As we recited it the tension in my hand eased and I knew I was coming out of trance. Suddenly, uncontrollably, my fingers flew open and the ring fell to the floor. It was just as if something had burst from a prison — released, free, and content. The oppressive atmosphere of the room was replaced by a sense of peace. To me it seemed that a light breeze swept through the place, and the rather stale air became fragrant with a sweet smell like that of fresh-cut flowers. It lingered just for a few seconds.

I looked at my companions. They had opened their eyes and unclasped their hands. For a moment or two they appeared a little dazed but there was evident relief on their faces. The pallor had gone from the man's face, and his wife, too, was a much healthier colour. 'I must bless your flat now', I said, and beginning with the bedroom I blessed

each room in turn. They followed me quietly and attentively as I did this. When I had finished I said: 'You will sleep
peacefully here from now on. You know that, don't you?'
They nodded and looked so relieved and happy, so different from the woebegone and tense couple they had been
when I first met them, that I was more than ever convinced
that a complete exorcism had been effected. Certainly
they did not need to call upon me again for this purpose,
but told me there was an entirely new atmosphere in their
flat from that day.

Outside when I left them the air was crisp and the light
of early dawn was filling the sky. The walk back home was
enjoyable but when I got back into bed just after four a.m.
I was utterly exhausted. The spiritual struggle of exorcism
can be extremely fatiguing and I find it necessary to relax
as soon as possible when it is over. If practicable I like to
sleep for an hour or two after commending my soul to
God. When I wake I feel marvellously refreshed,
invigorated, and buoyant.

17

AFTER THE FUNERAL

In the course of nearly thirty years in the ministry I have
conducted many funerals. Among them have been a number which concerned sudden death, murder, suicide, and
accidents ranging from airplane disasters to tripping over a
carpet. Most of these have had a peculiar atmosphere and
sometimes unusual sequels.

One was the funeral of a woman who, after a lengthy cor-
oner's inquiry, was judged to have died by her own hand.
From the very start I was struck by an extremely unpleasant
atmosphere which deepened as the service proceeded.
I could not fathom the reason for this. So far as outward
appearances went all those present in the chapel bore
expressions of genuine sorrow, deep concern, and suitable
attentiveness. Their behaviour could not have been faulted.
Because of that uneasy atmosphere, however, I found it
impossible to enter the condition of controlled trance
which I seek to achieve in order that my words may
convey more surely the psychic strength of hope and consolation. Had I been able to do so, I think that I might
have overcome the unhappy undercurrent.

A fortnight later I chanced to see one of the mourners
who had been present at the funeral. 'Sad business that,
Padre', he said. 'What did you think?' I must have looked
puzzled by his remark. 'You knew about the case?' he asked.
'I knew there had been an inquest and that the poor woman
took her own life', I replied. 'Was there any more than that?
Did they discover what made her do it?'

'It was all pretty mysterious', he answered. 'You see, I at-
tended the inquest. There was some suspicion that her husband may have caused her death. But there was insufficient

evidence about that and so the verdict of suicide was brought in. There was no doubt at all that she had had a rotten time of it for some years. I knew that. Personally I thought that he might have engineered her death. A queer fellow, you know. I've always thought so.'

'Well,' I said, 'we must not let our feelings be the judge. He must have gone through an awful time at the inquest and so we should be sorry for him.' 'Don't get me wrong, Padre', he broke in quickly. 'I'm not the sort to see the worst in a chap, or to gossip. But it does make you think, doesn't it, when you realize that there is talk of him selling up here and going off to marry another woman already.'

I thought it best not to pursue the matter but I could not help thinking about what he had said. The strange atmosphere during that funeral had been troubling me quite a bit since and I had reproached myself many times over my failure to break through it. Now I began to understand the reason for my disquiet in the light of what this man had now told me. I was to discover that the husband did indeed sell his house and move far away. Not an unnatural thing to do after such a tragedy. Many people, of course, find they cannot remain in a home where they have lost someone dear to them.

However, more than six months later, a man asked me to visit him with a view to exorcising his home. When he gave me the address I must say I was not surprised, nor sceptical of the genuineness of his story. For it transpired that he had bought the very house where the woman had ended her life. He had not been aware of the tragedy until some weeks after he had moved in. Then, in the course of conversation in a local shop in which he complained about the strange feeling the house gave him, someone told him what had happened there. Apparently one room in particular was most eerie. He was often conscious of a moaning sound and of shuffling noises for which there was no natural cause that he could observe. On the first occasion he had experienced these phenomena he told me the room felt so uncanny that his back became icy cold and his hair seemed to stand on end. He explained that he had never been one to believe in ghosts or hauntings but that this matter had so unnerved him that he had begun to consider moving out of the house. Then someone told him to contact me, as they knew I had been asked to conduct exorcisms in the district.

'You do believe me, Father?' He spoke most earnestly. 'I really have felt these things and heard them. It's just awful. I never thought there could be anything like this. If it went on and I were to stay here I think I would go out of my mind. Can you stop it?' 'Yes, of course I believe you', I said. 'These things do happen, more often than you might think. I ought to say though that *I* cannot put a stop, as you put it, to these manifestations. I am just the vehicle through which Jesus Christ, who is the Lord of the spiritual world, will bring peace to this unhappy soul. Show me where you are most conscious of these phenomena.'

He led me into the kitchen. It was rather dingy and ramshackle. 'Some of the furniture went with the house when I bought it', he explained. He pointed to a large upright wooden chair which stood by the old-fashioned open range. It was loaded with books and newspapers. 'I was sitting in that chair', he said, 'when I first had this trouble. I never feel right in it so I have piled it up like that.' Inwardly I thought that this was very likely to have been the chair which the dead woman had often used. His next words confirmed this. 'Neighbours have told me that the woman who died here was found in that chair. I suppose I ought to get rid of it.'

I asked him for a small basin of water and explained what I was about to do. 'I shall bless this water that God may use it to signify to us his mercy and the cleansing of all that is evil or unhappy. Then we shall pray that if there is a restless soul it may find his peace.' Having blessed the water in the name of the Father and of the Son and of the Holy Spirit I dipped my right thumb in it and made the sign of the cross on the lintels of each of the doors of the house with the invocation: 'Most merciful and loving Father, bless this home, and may all who enter it come in friendship and leave in peace. This is our prayer through Jesus Christ our Lord, Amen.'

Next, in the centre of each room I stood quietly with the man at my side. Making the sign of the cross I said: 'I speak in the name of God the Father who loves us eternally and in the power of Jesus Christ who has prepared a place for us in our Father's kingdom. If there be an unhappy soul who retains the agony of a bitter experience here, may you know the eternal compassion and understanding. If it be you (here I used the Christian name of the dead woman), I ask in the name of Jesus that you leave this place and go to that joyful abode which he has made ready for you. Go in peace and know him as the loving Lord of your spirit who will rejoice to receive you now.'

In each room I could sense very markedly some other presence than our own. When we came, last of all, back to the kitchen I glanced at the man. He looked very pale and serious but did not speak. Here the feeling of an unseen companion became so strong that I was positive that whoever it was must be deeply concerned in what was going on. Then that wooden chair riveted my attention in a most uncanny way. I felt a grip upon my forearm. This was so definite that I thought my companion had taken hold of me, but on glancing at him I saw his eyes were downcast and he had his hands clasped in front of him. That grip drew me towards the chair. When I was standing in front of it I experienced a decided drop in temperature. This chill made me feel very apprehensive. Tension began to build up in me to such a degree that I thought I would be forced to cry out in pain or fear.

I was certain now that it was here that the ghostly presence was seeking release. From the oppression of some terrible experience it had undergone? Scarcely knowing why, I sprinkled the chair and the floor round it with holy water and said: 'Distressed soul, I realize you have known a great torment. But do not be bound to this place. Your heavenly father knows and has infinite compassion for you. Enter then, with joy, the beautiful abode he has prepared for you.' As I spoke I felt I was spiritually struggling with a grievously restless person who needed to be convinced of the caring love of the Creator. It was as if I were exercising my faith in that love on that unhappy soul's behalf. I placed my hands above the chair, saying: 'Know now the peace of God and the companionship of Jesus Christ.' My hands then trembled so much that I thought I had lost control over them. Waves of coldness washed over me so that my breath came in deep gasps as if I were engaging in some fearful battle. I repeated the words several times. On each occasion I felt I was personally addressing the unseen presence. Then I asked the man if he would join me in the Lord's Prayer.

We recited it with great feeling and as we did so the tension in me relaxed. The strange chill also went and my hands became steady. I found very great comfort in the words 'and deliver us from evil', while the final phrase 'for thine is the kingdom, the power and the glory' came so freshly alive with its declaration of triumph that I knew a sudden transport of exultation. This was gloriously beautiful, just as one feels when a terrible burden has been lifted. And in that moment of sublime release, an invisible being passed beside me or out of me. I find it difficult to tell which. It was like the movement of a light breeze.

I turned to the man. He still looked pale and his eyes were rather glazed. 'Something's gone', he said, almost to himself. 'I believe so', I replied. 'I think there was an unhappy soul here wanting to communicate its distress. I hope you will find that now your home feels free.' He did not complain from that day of any further manifestations, and I am convinced that the exorcism was truly effective.

18

THE POWER IN SILENCE

It is no easy task to be the chaplain of a cemetery or crematorium. Certainly there is a special joy in such work. As well
as strengthening the clergyman's own faith, it can give him
the opportunity to present its hope and blessing to a captive
and ever-changing audience. It can provide a rich field for
pastoral work. But the responsibility is immense in these
days when the faith of multitudes is vague or non-existent,
because the chaplain must therefore seek to communicate to
the mourners the faith with which he himself is sustained.
This applies also to every mourner who does have the conviction of Christian faith. He or she must endeavour at the
deep level of the spirit-soul to arouse and even instil in the
others who are attending the funeral the consolation and
inspiration of that faith.

But how can this be done in the brief quarter of an hour
or so of the normal funeral service? I believe the answer lies
in the communication achieved through the extraordinary
power of silence. In it and through it a fellowship is established which transcends anything that can be achieved by
words. The spirit-to-spirit contact is the deepest we humans
can ever hope to have.

I have sensed on innumerable occasions at funerals and
by the bedsides of the sick how enriching for the spirit is
the simple act of silence. The fact is, of course, that our
thoughts and feelings cannot be encompassed in words, however beautiful these may contrive to be or however deeply
they are meant. Fellowship with one another, the most real
and tender fellowship, surpasses language. Heart calls to
heart as deep calls to deep. And it is in silence that we can
recollect our heavenly Father's love for us and thereby come

spiritually close to one another. We draw near because we are together in God, in whom all of us dwell.

At the beginning of every religious service and also during it we ought to have the opportunity to 'enter the silence'. The inscription, 'BE STILL AND KNOW THAT I AM GOD', was chosen by an actress friend to be carved on the gates of the communion rails in my London church. She gave them in memory of her young husband, an actor and promising playwright, who had lived courageously for some years in the knowledge that he had an incurable disease and who had died confident of God's eternal goodness and love. She chose the text because, as she said, 'In the silence God dwells. We had found that truth together, my husband and I. I want others to know it, the joy of it, and the nearness to one another that the silence brings. Perhaps when people kneel here for their Communion they will sense the beauty of being still and in that silence know that they are together in God.' So it is that when I visit those who are recently bereaved I seek a few moments of silence with them.

A father and mother had lost a twelve-year-old daughter through a brain haemorrhage. Jane was a lively, friendly, and highly intelligent child, very popular at school and a natural favourite with everyone. Her death was a shattering blow to her parents. At such a time one realizes only too well that words alone cannot bring comfort — certainly not a sermon on immortality nor even a reminder of the Christian hope and belief. In the hour of bereavement the heart can only respond to that deep compassionate yearning of the spirit which words can never express.

We stood together, the three of us, in the little front parlour respectfully darkened by its drawn blinds. The man was holding his wife's hand as he told me the circumstances of their daughter's death and arranged with me the details of the funeral. I let him speak on, for it was clearly a help for him to do so. When he paused at last I saw him squeeze her hand more tightly. I closed my own hand around their clasped ones and said: 'Shall we just be silent a little while? We can find God in the silence.'

And so we entered the silence, and as the stillness seemed to cloak around us there came calm and peace and assurance. In my heart I was saying: 'Father, we are with you now. Give to these dear people the consolation of your love for them. Help them to know that though Jane is beyond our present sight we are still together because we are forever in your presence.'

How long that silence continued I do not know. By the clock probably less than half a minute but by the spiritual measure we had touched eternity. Throughout this silent communication I told my spirit-soul to reach out to the spirit-souls of this grieving man and woman, to communicate to them the faith and hope that nourished me.

When these rich moments of stillness had ended I opened my eyes, and now it seemed that there was no room, no material object around the three of us. We appeared to be caught up in a beauty of such tenderness and radiance that I felt I could quite literally say that not only the immediate world about us but time itself was standing still. This experience could only have been momentary, but I believe it was also sensed by the husband and wife. Certainly what they said suggested that this was so.

'Thank you, Vicar', he said. 'Do you know, I felt something I have never known before. It was as if God was so real that nothing else mattered but him. And, you know, Jane was here, with us, and she was so happy. So very happy. Did you feel that?' he asked his wife. 'Yes, I did too', she replied, and there was a light of happy assurance in her eyes. 'Jane was so close, and I shall never worry or be sad again because I could see that she was happy.'

There are some who suspect and deplore the cult of Spiritualism. Certainly the orthodox Churches do. No doubt some will jump to the conclusion that I must be a Spiritualist. This is not so. But I do believe that because the Christian Church fails to emphasize enough the continuing and unbroken fellowship of the children of God, Spiritualism survives and gains its adherents, many of whom are also members of the orthodox Churches.

Yet the Christian Church acknowledges the Communion of Saints, the fellowship of those who have their faith and hope in Jesus Christ. That fellowship is indissoluble. Death cannot break it. Love, because it is of God, is eternal. Hence that rich and tender, compassionate and caring relationship which human beings have with each other cannot be thought of as temporal, something of this earth alone.

Over all those relationships where love dwells can be written, in words of blazing hope and glory, 'To be continued'. What we have known and loved here on earth which is good, true, and beautiful will be known and loved transcendently in the eternal world. I cannot believe, therefore, that the Church should be chary of our conscious attempt to remember our fellowship with those who have entered the unseen world nor be suspicious or doubtful of the benefit which comes when on rare occasions, usually soon after the death of someone we love, we are vouchsafed an experience of their presence. If we, like them, have set our hope in Jesus Christ, we are already in an eternal communion together by the very fact that our spiritual yearning is the same.

It is a wonderful help and inspiration to remember that others have had their way lit by the same hope and sustained by the same belief as our own, and though now in a greater light are yet one with us through our common faith in the Father God whom Jesus has revealed. Many have described to me how they have received intimations of the continuing life of their loved ones. These gave them much consolation and unforgettable reassurance but were always unsought, which is as it should be. It seems that this kind of revelation rarely, if ever, comes to people when they are beside themselves with grief or are purposely seeking some proof of their loved one's life in the unseen world. On the contrary, if this kind of perception arises at all it is when the mind is quiet and composed and there is no conscious desire for such experience.

All must be set aside so that the restlessness of the soul may cease and its waiting upon God become the one and only desire. Then comes the power which is in the silence.

19

TELEPATHY

A few years ago I gave some lectures on psychic phenomena which included one on telepathy. For several weeks I had not only given much thought to the preparation of this particular lecture but also discussed the subject a good deal with my wife and interested friends. In consequence the idea of telepathic communication was always very much on my mind.

Then one morning, when I was actually intending to write the lecture, I woke with a severe headache. This was very unusual for me, but the pain persisted for most of the early morning. It centred round the bridge of my nose and just between my eyes. In some strange way I felt that I should not seek relief, so I took nothing for it. An hour must have passed after this, and then I found myself suddenly thinking exclusively about my mother.

The image of her at home, nearly eighty miles away, persisted so vividly that I actually discovered myself talking aloud to her as if she were in my study with me. She appeared to be in bed and my father was standing beside her. There also seemed to be someone else present whom I could not make out clearly. This vision lasted only a few moments but recurred several times and made me most concerned about my mother's health. For an hour or two afterwards the pain in my forehead remained as a dull ache so that I could not concentrate on other matters. From time to time I found that I was conjuring up my mother's face. And on each occasion that it came to me clearly I would ask God to bless her.

It was when I was sitting at my desk glancing at my notes for the forthcoming lecture on telepathy that I felt compelled to close my eyes. Again my mother appeared to me quite distinctly. Once more I repeated my prayer for God to bless her, and this time there was an intense thumping between my eyes for a few seconds. It was so intense that I thought something must have burst inside my head. As suddenly as it started it ceased, and when it did so I felt something cold brush my face. It seemed to bathe my face with coolness and then I experienced a feeling of complete relief. The headache entirely lifted and I could scarcely believe the change that came flooding over me. I had the sense of something dangerous having left me. Three days later I received a letter from my father. In it he explained that my mother had suffered a severe haemorrhage. She had complained of very bad head pains when he had brought her an early morning cup of tea and in consequence she had remained in bed. An hour or so later her nose bled copiously. In the emergency my father contacted not only the doctor but a neighbour a few doors away who was a trained nurse. She was about to leave for duty at a local hospital, but came immediately and dealt with things very ably, applying ice from the refrigerator. By the time the doctor arrived the crisis was over.

My mother at that time, though still very active, was becoming rather frail, and the haemorrhage undoubtedly saved her life, or at least prevented what she would have hated, an incapacitating stroke. She was to be up and about again within a few weeks. I mention this matter because I believe that my concentration upon the subject of telepathy had opened up my psyche to encourage that very faculty, one which is an attribute of every human soul even though we rarely develop it or respond to it.

In order to exercise the faculties of the spirit-soul, some degree of trance is necessary, that is a condition in which we are least conscious of the physical needs and desires of our bodies. Most of us have known many occasions when we have appeared to be aware of someone's thoughts or intentions before they have actually told us of them. Perhaps the most common of these is the letter or telephone call which we had no real reason to expect and which comes soon after we were thinking of the writer or caller. If we analysed these incidents we would probably find that intuitions or perceptions of this kind came to us when we were either very mentally preoccupied or just daydreaming. In both cases we have temporarily shed, as it were, any real consciousness of our physical bodies so that the soul is ranging free and the spirit-soul is exercising more efficiently its own special faculties.

In the case of my mother's illness, my deep concentration upon the subject of telepathy had induced in me a condition which was particularly encouraging to semi-trance. And I was working on my lecture notes on the very day she would have been thinking specially of all her family because she thought she might not see them again. The psychic conditions being what they were, my spirit-soul could well have made communication with hers. The only area of questioning for me is the details of this experience.

I cannot be dogmatic about the interpretation of them but I can hazard a guess. Was the strange coldness that seemed to bathe my face a communicated awareness of the ice-packs applied to my mother's forehead? Was that other figure whom I could not clearly see in my vision actually the nurse who had come in to help? Or was I experiencing yet again what I have known at various times when I have stood beside a sick bed or, indeed, when I myself have been in danger, the ministration of an angelic being in response to my prayer for help?

One thing I know for sure since it was confirmed in later conversation with my parents. At the very hour when I felt my headache lift after those seconds of intense thumping, my mother had the haemorrhage which was to give her great relief, despite its unpleasantness, and bring her safely through a most critical time.

The day came for me to give the lecture on telepathy. An hour after I had done so I received a telephone call from someone who seldom sees us and normally telephones only twice a year, and never before at that particular time. Strangely enough, only a few minutes before I had mentioned to my wife that we should ourselves contact him. 'How very extraordinary', I said. 'I was about to phone you! And I have just returned from church after giving an address on telepathy!'

'Telepathy!' he exclaimed. 'Certainly I believe in it. Just listen to this. My daughter has just been on the line. She's been in America for the last few months, and didn't know I have recently had a serious operation. We didn't tell her because it would have upset her. We are all very close, and we knew she would have felt she ought to take the next plane home. Anyway, she sensed on the day I was taken to the hospital that I was ill, and kept mentioning this to her employers. In the end it was they who advised her to telephone us today and find out. What makes me more sure of telepathy between us is the fact that she had never known me to have a day's illness and there was no suspicion of anything wrong with me when she left for America. I still wrote her my usual weekly letter but always got my wife to post it for me as if it came from home. I must say I was thinking a lot about her while I was in hospital so I believe our thoughts crossed. Certainly I believe in telepathy.'

The following Sunday I was still thinking a lot about telepathy, and wondering particularly about its usefulness for acquiring knowledge of those who might be in special need of prayer and consolation. During Morning and Evening Prayer I always conduct the intercessionary prayers from the centre of the nave. In this place, by having my people round me, I sense much more strongly the feeling or atmosphere of such prayer, which is more intimate and topical than the formal, set prayers of the rest of these services.

Usually I begin by asking that 'we enter now into the quietness together and allow to pervade our being the peace of this holy place'. Sometimes I will add that we are doing in our time what those before us in that house of prayer have done down the years. In this way we are made conscious of our unity and continuity with all who have sought to live by faith in Christ, and so the psychological factors which stimulate the reality and power of corporate prayer are aroused.

After holding this quietness for a few moments I am aware that I have entered what I can best describe as a controlled trance. Although I am perfectly aware of the carefully prepared themes of prayer with which I plan to lead the congregation, yet I know my spirit-soul is almost ranging free. I have, therefore, become wide open to spiritual forces beyond myself. Since we have acknowledged the Lordship of Christ and our dependence upon him, those forces will be according to his will and not alien to it as might well be the case if we sought trance without first referring our souls to his guidance.

I believe this is why time and again I have injected spontaneous phrases into these prayers and sometimes wholly discarded my prepared themes for others entirely different. In other words, the free movement of the Spirit of God has not been inhibited by keeping rigidly to a preset pattern of prayer. It has long ago ceased to surprise me that members of the congregation tell me after a service that they did not understand how I could have known their particular need, sorrow, or perplexity, because one of my intercessions was so absolutely right and helpful for them. In every case this had been a prayer added by me and not among those I had previously prepared and selected. The explanation, I believe, is that in the condition of controlled trance my spirit-soul is functioning almost as pure spirit and therefore I am receiving the strong desires of certain members of my congregation. We call this faculty telepathy.

On this particular Sunday during the period of quiet I suddenly found my attention being directed to some red paintwork which had been applied to the lower brick of the walls of the church by a former churchwarden several years before. It had been his farewell gift of service to the church he loved before he and his family emigrated to New Zealand. It seemed a completely irrelevant thing to occupy my attention and it made me feel somewhat guilty to think I should allow such a distraction at so important a time. But that painted brickwork continued to rivet me. I began to see him quite distinctly in my mind's eye. This experience could only have lasted for a few moments, and I made a determined effort to thrust aside such reverie and proceed with the prayers I had prepared.

I began with a prayer for the peace of the world. But mention of the world conjured up the idea of New Zealand and forced me back again to that red paint and my former churchwarden. What followed that prayer for world peace rose up from very deep within me and without conscious reflection. It went something like this: 'Shall we give thought to those who have worshipped with us in past years and have served our church well? We ought not to forget them and what we owe to them. Most of us will remember Mr Rodwell and his family who emigrated to New Zealand four years ago. Let us remember them now for they need our prayers at this time.'

I could not tell why I uttered that last sentence and particularly that final phrase. It just seemed to be wrung from me. The same power which had me in control urged me on to follow up with one of my favourite prayers: 'O heavenly Father, we thank thee for the great blessing of family and friends. Surround them and us with the circle of thy divine protection, and may we see in the life that we share together that thou art giving to us a foretaste of the beauty of thy eternal kingdom.'

I then went on: 'We remember before thee, too, all our friends who have left our parish or, like the Rodwells, have moved to other lands. We know they are still one with us in thy fellowship. Thou seest their present needs. In the assurance of thy love we commend them to thee that they may be ever strengthened, comforted, and guided by thy Spirit. May they receive thy healing in this hour. Through Jesus Christ, who is our Lord and theirs. Amen.'

That last petition arose so strongly that I felt compelled

to express it. In the mental image I had of Mr Rodwell I perceived such anxiety that I was convinced there was illness in his family. This was the first time I had mentioned the family by name in a church service for four years, and I had certainly not thought about them particularly or heard from them for many months past. This concern about them, however, persisted throughout that Sunday so I repeated the intercession for them at the evening service. I continued to think about telepathy and now began associating it with this strange compulsion to pray for this family. I began to wonder what it meant.

A fortnight later I was to know, for I received an airmail letter from Mr Rodwell saying that his wife had been taken suddenly and critically ill. He was so distressed that he had prayed as never before. 'I remember, Vicar,' he wrote, 'how you taught us to pray and I prayed like that. I thought of you and of those prayers you take in the middle of the church. And I found it helped. It was last Sunday I prayed like that and I felt you were all with us. Now, thank God, she has come safely through. It is like a miracle.'

The Sunday he had prayed so earnestly was the very one on which I had been constrained to remember his family in those intercessionary prayers.

20

STRANGE COMMUNICATION

It can sometimes be difficult to distinguish between precognition and telepathic communication from the unseen world. A case in point happened several years after I had taken the burial service of a person who had been a close friend of a well-known clairvoyant. The latter had taken me aside after the service to express his appreciation of the way the service had been conducted. He was particularly grateful for certain comments I had made.

'It was not', he declared, 'too wretchedly orthodox. I entirely agree with everything you said, and the view you take of death.' I had never met him until then though I recognized him from a television programme I had seen some months earlier. Before the week was out he wrote me a warm-hearted letter reiterating his gratitude for the comfort and help which his friend's funeral had given him. I sent back a suitable reply. With this our contact and correspondence ceased, although from time to time we would catch sight of each other in a London street or store and smile or wave in recognition.

Then came the day, about five years later, when I was clearing out my desk and came across his letter again. It arrested my attention so much that the events of the funeral came vividly back to my mind and I thought of that conversation I had had with him. In the light of what followed I cannot think it was pure coincidence that the very next morning I noticed a headline in my daily newspaper. It stated that the clairvoyant had died while on a very successful tour of the Far East.

I read the short account of his life with great interest. There was also a photograph of him. It was this which began to exercise an extraordinary fascination over me. It was not a particularly good likeness but nevertheless had something about it which appeared to bring him to life before my mind's eye. Several times during the day I felt drawn to look at it again. On each occasion I had a clear mental image of the man as he had spoken to me those five years ago. This impression became even more vivid as the day wore on.

Towards evening I picked up the paper again and once more turned to the photograph. I felt under some strange compulsion to do so, as if I were being hypnotized by it. It then occurred to me that my attention was being focussed in this way in order that I might receive some information, perhaps a message from him. So I settled myself quietly in an easy chair with the paper spread on my knees and continued looking at the photograph. At the same time I completely relaxed my body, concentrating upon each limb and urging it to respond to the thought of complete stillness. When all tensions in me were thus consciously overcome I sought to make the photograph come alive by dwelling upon the memory of that day five years ago when the clairvoyant and I had talked.

As I continued to gaze at the photograph it became misty. Then a peculiar thing happened. Superimposed on it I saw what I can only call the living face of the man as I had known him from our brief encounter. Now it seemed as if he were in the room with me. Then I heard a voice saying: 'You will be taking my funeral service. I tell you now so that you may be prepared.' No further message came to me, but I was completely convinced there and then that I would indeed conduct the service for him.

It was no great surprise, therefore, when a friend of his telephoned a few days later wanting to consult me about the form and details of the funeral which he had been made responsible for arranging at a nearby crematorium. While I happened to be a member of the team of clergy who regularly officiated at that crematorium it was surely not coincidence that the service should have been arranged on the particular day of the week when I usually took duty there. There were several other clergy to whom on that day it might have been allocated. There had been no instructions, written or otherwise, left by the clairvoyant that I should be specially requested to officiate.

For all I knew when I first read the account of the man's death, his funeral could well have been arranged elsewhere. Out of London, maybe, or even, under the circumstances, abroad. It might also have been a burial and not a cremation. These facts, together with the psychic phenomena associated with the photograph, incline me to believe that he not only desired me to be responsible for conducting his funeral but that his spirit-soul was, in some mysterious way, working to that end. By concentrating upon that newspaper picture and recalling vividly a five-year-old memory I had entered a stage of trance in which my spirit-soul would be receptive to that of another. At the same time peculiar spiritual forces created the particular situation which ensured that I should be the officiating minister.

A somewhat similar case occurred when I saw the Press announcement of the death, in tragic circumstances, of a popular actor. Immediately I felt a sense of almost personal loss for I had always enjoyed immensely his clever characterizations on television.

As I read and reread the brief obituary I began to have the most powerful yearning to bring comfort to his family and friends. Even as I felt this I perceived that I would be allowed that privilege and became convinced that it would be through conducting his funeral. I had no reason to think this could happen. I had never met him and he was not a parishioner of mine though it chanced we lived in the same very large London borough. For all I knew he might have been of some other denomination than Church of England and his funeral could have taken place anywhere, even out of London. But my premonition continued throughout that day and the next. I was so convinced by it that I scribbled a few lines about what should be specially said at the service, for

117

which I found some of the newspaper details helpful.

I always like to know as much as possible about a deceased person because otherwise funerals in a great city can become very impersonal affairs. In the vast population of London it is hardly possible for a clergyman to have had intimate contact in every case with either the deceased or the bereaved. Any information, however sketchy, is invaluable in helping to bring to the funeral service a real feeling of intimacy and contact which will deepen the spirituality of the occasion for all concerned.

A few days after reading the newspaper announcement I received a call from a relative of the dead actor wishing to discuss details of the funeral, which had been arranged at a cemetery where I was then acting as chaplain. Though it is true most funerals which took place there would have been taken by me the fact is that only a very small percentage of those dying in that borough are nowadays buried there. There are, therefore, several factors in this case also which suggest that it could hardly be one of pure coincidence. On the contrary I believe I had been given a genuine premonition of my involvement in the matter and that here again spiritual forces were at work to ensure that my deep longing to bring comfort to the bereaved was realized.

In those two cases there was ample opportunity for the reflection which encourages extra-sensory perception. It appears, however, that this is not always necessary; I was requested at only a few hours' notice to conduct the funeral of a lady who had died at the age of ninety-eight. Owing to a previous engagement I could only arrive for this service a minute or so early. I noticed that there was a fairly large congregation already assembled and waiting for me, and unlike most funerals of people of great age many there were quite young. The general impression, too, was that they came from an artistic background. I wondered if the dead lady might have been in the theatre, but then thought no more of it.

I knew nothing about her except her name and her age.

Owing to the rush to get there on time I had completely forgotten to ask the undertaker for any details about her, but he had told me that her sister was one of the mourners. It was during the reading of the twenty-third psalm that my attention was momentarily distracted by the sound of a piano. It seemed far away and though so brief the music impressed me as being both thrilling and ethereal. I realized that this was a psychic experience and that what I had heard was purely in my own head.

When the psalm ended I spoke for a minute or two, as is my custom, about the Christian concept of death as the way through to a new creation. But all the while that snatch of strange music stirred an almost feverish turmoil of questioning in the back of my mind. Why had I heard it? What could it mean? These thoughts became so distracting that I had to make a determined effort to set them aside when I led the congregation in the prayers that followed. But psychic phenomena are not easily forgotten or dismissed. Coming up through my concentration I repeatedly got the image of a piano, and towards the close of the prayers I found myself adding: '. . . and we would thank thee, Lord, for the precious joy of music which so lifts the hearts of men; and for that great talent for performing it with which thou blessed our beloved Sarah (the name of the dead woman). For all the pleasure she thus gave to so many we do most gratefully rejoice.'

When the service was over several people came up and thanked me and in particular for that added prayer. The sister asked me if I had ever heard the dead woman play. 'Somewhat before your time, I should think', she said with a smile when I admitted that I had not done so. But she was clearly delighted that I had mentioned her sister's ability and obviously thought that I knew all about it. Under the circumstances I felt I could not tell her that my knowledge had only come in an inspired flash during the service. From conversation round us I gathered that she had been a pianist of some prominence many years earlier. Her name had certainly meant nothing to me and I can only hazard the following guess as to the reason for my strange enlightenment.

I had just left a rather exhausting previous engagement and had driven to the cemetery in the most trying traffic conditions. During that journey my eye was constantly on the clock and I became increasingly concerned with every hold-up as to whether I should be late for the funeral. Lateness for any service, and particularly for a funeral, is absolute anathema to me and I have always done everything in my power to avoid it.

Consequently there must have been a great build-up of nervous tension and anxiety. In some instances such pressure results in a trance state when the tension ends or is successfully resolved. There is such a blissful release that the spirit-soul rejoices and may then exercise its peculiar powers. And I had just such a sense of relief when I managed to arrive on time for the service.

21

PREMONITIONS

On several occasions I have received psychic impressions while conducting church services. I do not find this surprising, for when one is engaged in such an intensely spiritual task one is closely in tune with the realm of the spirit. The great concentration required also helps to facilitate the working of the faculties of the spirit-soul by inducing a level of trance.

I recall an instance when a very devout elderly couple came to the altar rail to receive Communion. The husband had recently had a major operation, but he made light of it and, with indomitable courage, shortly after leaving hospital resumed the steadfast, lifetime habit of attending the early morning Sunday celebration of Holy Communion. His wife always came with him. On this particular Sunday as I brought them the bread and wine of the Sacrament, my attention was arrested by observing an aura of bright light which shone round their heads. It was so very beautiful, and conveyed such an exquisite sense of peace, that I trembled with excitement and emotion when I approached them.

I wondered what it meant. Then, in the very act of raising the chalice to the lips of the quietly kneeling woman, I had the feeling that her earthly life was close to its end. This puzzled me as, although the long strain of her husband's illness had affected her own health, she had always seemed so cheerful that I imagined he was more likely to die before her. Because of this I thought at first that my intuition must be wrong and that it really applied to him. As I ministered the Sacrament to them both I gave special thanks in my heart for their wonderful example of love during more than fifty years of married life and of their unceasing devotion to our Lord in his Church.

I always stand in the porch after a service to say good-bye to the worshippers and on this occasion I shook hands with this couple with an added warmth, inwardly saying a prayer for them and for the continuing comfort which I knew they brought to each other. It so happened that my wife and I were leaving that same Sunday evening to fly to Nice for a month's holiday duty in the English Church there. As I watched that dear couple, so like Darby and Joan, go out of the church gate arm in arm, I had a catch in my throat and tears in my eyes. I was certain that it would be the last time I should see them together.

When I turned back into the church this impression became so powerful that I was impelled to go back to the gate again and watch them walk on. Only when they were out of sight did I return to the sanctuary, where I knelt for some minutes reflecting upon my experience during the recent Communion service, and holding vividly in my mind the charming but poignant picture of that fine old couple leaving the church which meant so much to them.

About ten days later in the Chaplain's house in Nice I was awakened during the early hours by what I thought were footsteps on the marble staircase just outside the door. As only my wife and myself were in the house I thought at first there must be an intruder. I became wide awake and listened more intently. The steps were light, almost gliding, but not in the least furtive. I had the feeling that someone had entered our room and was standing by my bed. I now realized the presence was a spiritual one, and quite involuntarily I sat upright and a sound was forced from my lips. My wife afterwards told me it was as if I had called out the Christian name of the wife of the couple I have mentioned.

The presence lingered by me for some seconds after this. Far from upsetting me, it was the very reverse, soothing and infinitely happy. It reminded me of my experience during that Communion service two Sundays before. My mind linked this with the present psychic phenomenon and I was fully convinced that the wife had just died or was about to do so. My premonition proved correct, for we received an urgent trunk call next morning from my secretary in London to say that the wife had died during that night and asking me to suggest who should take her funeral if I was unable to return to England to do so.

It was also during a celebration of Holy Communion, when I was saying the Prayer for the Church, that I had another premonition of death. At that time my mother-in-law was in hospital in Portsmouth. My wife had just spent a week there visiting her daily, and had returned heartened by the success of an operation performed on her mother.

In the quiet moments when the congregation can reflect individually upon their families during the Prayer for the Church, I had naturally given special thought to my wife's mother. As I was praying for her I suddenly sensed a presence at my side. I half turned and saw a tall, shadowy figure standing near me. I could not distinguish any features as the apparition was wraithlike and did not remain long after I had noticed it. It disappeared but I continued to feel its presence throughout the remainder of the service. Afterwards my server, an elderly man, asked me if I had seen a tall ghost standing by me during the administration. He was quite convinced that a spiritual presence had manifested itself, and in the end I had to confess to him what I had myself experienced.

When I returned to the vicarage, my wife said that she had heard a voice calling her name several times while I was taking that service. Once, because it sounded so clear, she thought it must be someone calling to a child of the same name in the road outside, but there was no one about. When I told her of my own experience, we reached the conclusion that perhaps her mother had communicated with us in the spirit. She was, incidentally, a woman of over average height.

Even as we were comparing notes the telephone rang and the sister from the hospital informed my wife that her mother had taken a sudden turn for the worse. Perhaps she would wish to come at once, if this were possible? I now realized that it was likely that the spirit-soul of my mother-in-law *had* been liberated in her state of final coma and had communicated with us. I said to my wife, who was perplexed over what to do, 'Mother will be dead within three hours. I know it. You cannot possibly reach her by train in that time. I think it would be best if we gave ourselves a chance to think quietly and prayerfully about her during that period. There is nothing better now that either of us can do.' Three hours later, almost to the minute, the telephone rang. Again it was the ward sister on the line: 'Your mother has just died. It was quite peaceful.'

Another instance of premonition associated with death occurred when my wife and I were in France. I had been asked to take a Sunday morning service during an interregnum at the English Church in Cannes.

Just before the service two strangers, a man and wife who were on holiday, spoke to me about a road accident. They had arrived on the scene just after it had happened. Two cars had been in collision, and they noticed that the most seriously damaged had an English registration. As fellow countrymen they had pulled up to see if they could be of any special help. One of the occupants of the English car, a young woman, had been killed, and they wondered if they should be the ones gently to inform the parents at home in England.

However, the French police had naturally taken everything well in hand, and there appeared nothing that the couple could do. So, realizing what a terrible shock the news of their daughter's death would be for them, they asked me if I would remember the parents during prayers. I therefore offered a prayer for the comfort and consolation of this stricken father and mother in the intercessions. As I said this prayer I became aware of a strange feeling that it was incumbent upon me in some way to be specially involved in the tragedy.

I still had a fortnight of further holiday before my return to England, and during that time I had the recurring sense that there was something I was being asked to do. It became a kind of burden upon me, although I could not see what it might be or indeed how I could be concerned in something which had happened hundreds of miles away to people whom I had never met. But the strange feeling of some kind of involvement persisted no matter how hard I tried to reason myself out of it.

Then a few nights later in Nice I had a dream in which I saw myself conducting the funeral of the young woman, and at the same time being relieved of my burden in this matter. It was thus made clear to me that I would be the medium of comfort to those bereaved parents through the funeral of their daughter.

On the face of it my taking that funeral was highly unlikely. I did not know the parents nor even their exact address, simply that they lived somewhere in London. Certainly they did not know me, nor that I had prayed for them in a church in the south of France shortly after their daughter had been killed. It was also probable that the family were not even Church of England. Nevertheless I could not shake off this peculiar premonition that I would have this special contact with them. When I returned to England I found that the very first funeral at which I had been scheduled to officiate, as duty clergyman for that day at a well-known crematorium, was this young woman's.

Yet another example of premonition, also during an act of worship in church, occurred during a Christmas Carol Service held by candlelight. Three evenings before it took place, my wife and I were coping with addressing about three hundred Christmas cards. In the middle of this task I remarked upon one of the names on our list of friends to whom we always send the season's greetings.

Usually we received a card from this friend rather early in December and the fact that we had not yet heard from her arrested my attention. I said to my wife that I thought she must be ill. She was now elderly, very dear to us, and had always been deeply interested in my ministry since the days when I had served in her parish as a curate ten years before. The impression that she must be unwell continued to recur to me more and more, but owing to the pressure of engagements I did not telephone to inquire after her. I decided I would do so after the Carol Service was over.

When the day came there was a very large congregation; every pew was filled and many people had to stand. It might be thought that at such a time and in such a crowd psychic experience would be unlikely. Even more so because I had to be very much on my toes to ensure that the service went off without a hitch. It was an unusual and rather complicated one, with several professional actors, singers, and musicians taking part. Indeed I was completely concentrated upon achieving the maximum smoothness and artistic excellence of this very exciting act of praise and thanksgiving for the wonder of Christmas. No doubt this very concentration caused the working in me of extra-sensory perception by inducing a measure of trance.

The service had reached a highly moving and beautiful climax through the profoundly passionate singing of a West Indian. Then I moved to the lectern to read the final lesson. The atmosphere was now highly charged with psychic force, enhanced by the soft radiance of hundreds of candles and the impressive silence of that great crowd packed into every corner of the church. I was gripped by the awe of the occasion. My spirit bounded at the high privilege of crowning the marvel of this exhilarating act of worship by proclaiming the opening verses of St John's Gospel in which he unfolds the glory of the incarnation.

The wonderful inspiration of the evening had lifted me into what can only be described as a mystical state. I felt, as never before, that the Spirit of God would declare himself through the passage I was about to read. And as I read I was aware of a tremendous power exultantly pouring through me. My voice was not my own but an instrument of the Church Triumphant. I saw that all of us in that crowded building were in the stream of eternity, truly part of the

126

universal family of God's people. Time was swallowed up. Christians of the first days and of the present and of the everlasting future — all were caught up in one great mystic union. I felt we were truly sharing the presence of angels and archangels and all the company of heaven.

I reached the passage: '. . . as many as received him to them gave he power to become the sons of God, even to them that believe on his name. . .'. It was during these words of glorious promise that I saw a pale white shape just in front of the lectern. It seemed to be deliberately attracting my attention and was so arresting that I paused in my reading. Into my mind flashed the sudden thought that the spirit of someone known to me had just passed through the veil of death. I then distinctly heard the word 'Eveline'.

I did not find this perception at all daunting but rather, after my hesitation (which despite its brevity could not have gone unnoticed by that large congregation), it seemed to give even deeper insight and comfort to the closing words of the lesson: 'And the Word was made flesh and dwelt among us, and we beheld his glory, the glory as of the Only-begotten of the Father, full of grace and truth.' I felt that the apparition was underlining for me the amazing power and glory of God which had come into the world in Jesus Christ. It was as if it had said to me: 'What you are reading now is the very truth. I can tell you it is, for *now I know it*.'

When the service was over the wife of my churchwarden took me aside. 'Vicar', she said, and her voice was trembling with emotion, 'when you paused in that lesson I saw a being like an angel standing in front of you. Then it passed quite close to me. I believe you saw it too.' She had been seated in the front pew only a few feet from the lectern. She was a very serious person not given to flights of fancy.

During the week that followed we received the news of the death of our old friend. She had died in the early evening of that Sunday of the Carol Service at the very time when it was drawing to a close and I was reading that lesson. Her name was Eveline.

22

PRECOGNITION

At one time my wife and I lived in a vicarage only thirty yards or so from a busy main road. At the west end of the church there is an almost right-angle corner as the road follows the border of what is the remnant of an old village green. This sharp bend is a hazard to traffic as it is so unexpected, and many drivers tend to ignore the warning signs as they approach it at too great a speed.

When we first moved in we would hear late at night and in the early hours the squeal of brakes as drivers suddenly realized the danger. Almost every week-end there would be accidents of varying seriousness. It was not unusual to be startled from our sleep by the grinding crash of metal and the splintering of glass when cars skidded on taking the bend. Some would plough on through iron railings which enclosed the green or collide with the pillars of a crossing-island.

After enduring these night-time shocks for nearly eighteen months, with their constant accompaniment of scrambling from bed to see if help were needed, it occurred to me that I should start praying for the safety of motorists on this particular stretch. Consequently, whenever I walked past it I would send up an arrow prayer for angelic protection to be accorded to them.

About this time a young couple visited us and were accompanied by the young man's mother. It transpired during conversation that she was an exceptionally good medium. She mentioned that on passing the village green she sensed that it had a rather evil psychic atmosphere. She had never seen it before and knew nothing of its early history. I was able to tell her that a century ago it had been an area where known criminals and other bad characters congregated, particularly on public holidays. Old records mention the sordid behaviour and even murder associated with it. Incidentally the day she saw it was fine and sunny, when it was looking its most attractive.

I too had become aware of an unpleasant feeling about the place, sometimes amounting to a positive apprehension, especially if I took the short-cut through the middle of the green after dark. I now recalled with special significance the various tragedies which had occurred in the vicinity, including some violent ones during my own time in the parish. So besides offering prayer for the safety of road-users, I began to pray also that any evil forces lingering in the area of the green should be exorcized. I asked for angels to care for it and guard it. Gradually but quite perceptibly after this regular intercession I noted that our week-ends were less and less disturbed and accidents became rare. I began to give thanks now whenever I passed that way for what I felt must be the answer to my prayers.

Then, about midnight one Saturday, my wife and I were abruptly awakened by the scream of brakes and tyres followed by the noisy bump of metal. 'Oh dear,' I sighed, 'I suppose we are going back to one of those nights again.' I felt too exhausted to get up immediately to see if help might be required and was grateful to hear an engine start up soon afterwards. Clearly no one had been injured and I tried to get back to sleep, but first I made a prayer for God's protection on those who would round that precarious corner during the rest of the night. I did this by first creating a clear mental picture of the area and then commending it to the care of his angels.

It was difficult to sleep after that interruption, but nearly two hours later I was on the border of unconsciousness when I had a strange vision. I saw what was obviously the aftermath of an accident in which three cars had been involved. A group of young people, including some who were dark-skinned and a girl with long, very fair hair, were wandering about, evidently in a daze. Other people were lying in the

F
129

road and I was standing among them. Then the scene changed to the inside of the vicarage, where I was surrounded by the victims of the accident and there was a good deal of blood everywhere. Some held their heads in their hands and seemed to be badly injured, and I was doing what I could for them.

The whole thing seemed so very real that it brought me back quite forcefully to full consciousness. For a while I lay thinking about it until gradually the mental picture dissolved and I made yet another prayer, but this time more precisely and thoughtfully, for God's care and protection upon the traffic outside. I also tried to take up the whole scene of that nightmarish vision into his care. After this I felt calmer and the distress aroused by the strong sense of reality of the experience was relieved.

Now I did fall asleep, but not for long. The luminous figures on the bedside clock showed it to be little more than an hour later when we were awakened by another scream of tyres followed by a series of grinding crashes. We could hear the sound of buckling metal and the shatter of glass which continued for several long and sickening seconds. We were both so shocked that for some moments we lay quite rigid in bed, hearts palpitating and hardly daring to move. Then came the sound of a female voice crying out: 'Oh, help us. Help us, please help us, somebody.'

I was out of bed then with all speed. Stumbling into slippers and dressing-gown and seizing an electric torch I raced out of the front door towards that dreaded corner. But as I looked towards it I could not believe my eyes. There was no sign of an accident! I was so nonplussed that I stopped dead in my tracks not knowing what to do. Could it have been a dream?

Then I turned the corner and saw a scene resembling the one I had observed in the dream which had awakened me earlier. Three cars were sprawled across the road and a number of young people were standing, obviously dazed by shock, in the midst of the confusion. Several of them were coloured people and one was holding his face in his hands. Between his fingers blood was pouring. A young white girl with long, fair hair was standing by another vehicle. She was stock-still and staring glassily into space, evidently still in shock.

The obvious thing was to get everyone into the vicarage while I telephoned for an ambulance, and then to minister what first aid I could to the ones who had received the worst injuries. After the first few minutes of this intense activity I was able to reflect a little. It struck me how very similar the scene had now become to what I had been shown in that strange vision an hour ago. Several details agreed. Three cars had been involved in the accident; some of their occupants were coloured, and there was a girl with long fair hair. There were coloured, and there was a girl with long fair hair. There was also a lot of blood dripping from several superficial face thing that did not fit was the actual site of the accident. Though my vision did not offer me a clear idea of this I had presumed it to be at the bend in the road where other accidents had been in the past. Instead it was thirty or forty yards *before* it.

Those prayers for protection which I had regularly made for that corner had been effective. Though there had been an accident it was not at that particular spot but some distance from it. Moreover, it did not prove too serious. No one had to be detained in hospital. All had been answered — the prayer for protection, the prayer for the care of the angels, and the prayer for compassion.

When I recall the apparent severity of the accident which had been conjured in my half-awakened state an hour earlier, I ask myself: if I had not made the prayer I did at that time, would that accident have proved much worse than it actually was? After all, the three cars had sustained a good deal of damage and one of them was so badly battered it had to be towed away. It seemed a miracle that no one was seriously injured.

I believe my premonition was an example of the

131

perception which the spirit-soul can exercise when it is partially freed by a condition of trance. Such, no doubt, was the state I must have been in due to my uneasy sleep after that first alarming crash had awakened me earlier that night. When we hover on the border of sleep, the spirit-soul is active and extra-sensory perception is heightened. So can come our premonitions.

23

PETS AND PSYCHIC EXPERIENCE

Pet lovers have often asked if I have had any psychic experiences which concerned animals. There have, indeed, been several, two of which are noteworthy. Both were to do with pets, a dog and a cat, which had lived with us for a good many years.

One day Judy fell ill. She was a beautiful liver-and-white spaniel, a parting present from the parish where I had served my first curacy. She had to have an operation to remove some tumours, and the vet warned us that owing to her age she might not survive it. We were deeply saddened by this news, for she had been a wonderful companion and had gone almost everywhere with us. With heavy hearts we left her in the surgery and returned home. Hardly able to see through tear-dimmed eyes we entered the house. It seemed so empty, with Judy's basket a poignant reminder.

At the hour we had been told she would be undergoing the operation, we went into the church. Together we knelt at the altar rail and prayed silently. After several minutes of quiet I began to say a prayer aloud: 'O heavenly Father, we thank thee for all the pleasure Judy has given us over the years. We thank thee for all the memories we treasure of her companionship in our various homes and parishes. We love her, Lord, so dearly, and delight so much in her special ways . . . We remember . . . '. A whole stream of memories began to flow and I recited them aloud out of the fullness of my heart. 'Now, dear Lord, as she undergoes this operation, give skill to the vet and grant her thy healing.'

Through my mind there continued to pass a series of flash-back pictures of our outings with Judy. Now what I could see was not the poor limp creature we had just left in the surgery but Judy in the fullness of her powers. Walks on Hampstead Heath, in the streets and parks of Westminster and Blackheath during the days of my curacies, and along country lanes around Royal Air Force stations where I had served as a chaplain. All appeared vividly and as if they had taken place but yesterday.

Finally I could see her again as we had left her on the surgeon's table, her soulful eyes staring at us so forlornly, her body sadly showing the thinning signs of the tumours. Her pathetic whimper when she saw us depart seemed to sound still in my ears. I tried to pray aloud again but no words would come through the heartache. I reached out to take my wife's hand and held it to find comfort between us. Her lips were moving in silent prayer. Her face was wet with tears.

Then it happened. I had turned my gaze upon the altar and there, over it, I saw the phantom of a large white dog. In appearance it resembled a huge Alsatian. It was splendidly regal, motionless, its coat of a dazzling brightness and pure white, like snow. I stared at it, spellbound. The vision remained for several seconds, glowing and iridescent, and during that time it aroused a great sense of hope within me. Now I *knew* Judy would be all right. Something about the vision certified her recovery.

In great elation I told my wife. 'Judy will be O.K. . . . I know it', I said. 'Perhaps you won't believe it but I have just seen an apparition, or a vision, or something of that kind, of a great white dog. It was over the altar. Maybe dogs have their own angels. Why not? Anyway it has convinced me that we shall hear good news of her.' And sure enough, Judy was duly restored to us and lived on actively for another two years, dying at last at the ripe old age of fourteen.

There was an interesting sequel when nearly a year later I mentioned this experience to friends. They listened attentively and afterwards the wife said: 'Strange you should speak of this today because I have with me a little book which I only bought this morning.' She produced it and there on the cover was an artist's impression of a large white dog which the author alleged he had seen and which he believed to be a 'spirit-guide'. Evidently the book had been written by a Spiritualist. The dog was like a large white Alsatian similar to the figure I had seen over the altar of my church. It was even depicted facing the same way as the one in my vision.

I have often reflected upon this matter and have come to the conclusion that it is not outrageous or impossible to believe in a transcendent (or transfigured) animal creation which could have meaning for that which is in this world. St Paul indeed envisaged that all creation will be transformed, and not simply the human part of it, in what he called the 'new creation'.

The other case concerned our cat, Satan, a beautiful black Persian who had been a lovable companion to us for eighteen years. He had joined our household as a kitten, almost at the same time as did Judy, to whom he was quite devoted. Probably because of her companionship he exhibited a number of dog-like ways, accompanying her on her walks with us.

Towards the end of his life he became afflicted with a disease of the kidneys so that he rapidly faded to a shadow of his former glossy self. Dehydration made him just skin and bones, and though some treatment gave a little relief for a week or two it was very clear that we must make the decision to have him put to sleep to save him further suffering. It was a heartbreaking decision, and when the vet came to collect him we felt as if we had lost something very precious which had given great joy in our life through those eighteen years. We sat almost in silence for nearly two hours after Satan had been taken away knowing that sometime during that period he would be put to sleep.

At length we walked out together into the garden, reminding ourselves of how much our pet had loved it, climbing its trees, hiding in its bushes and then bounding from them immediately he heard us whistle for him. We thought of him basking on the lawn in the warmth of summer days and frisking quaintly in the occasional snow of winter. We recalled how at the ending of each day he would sit patiently on the

sill of the kitchen window for one of us to let him indoors
for the night.

'Let us say a prayer for him', I said. 'Do you remember
the time we took him and Judy to church for the Pets' Service? And what about that "angel" dog I saw over the altar
when Judy was so ill? It is surely right that we should remember him before our heavenly Father.' We went back into the house and while we looked out of the window together I said a prayer of thanks to God for the blessing he
had given us in this little creature, and asked that he should
know the joy of life in the 'new creation'.

'Do you think there is a life hereafter for animals?' my
wife asked me. 'I think I do.' 'I cannot see why not', I replied. 'Our little Satan was the subject of our love and care
and he reciprocated by giving us companionship. The proof
of that is in the fact that we miss him so. Yes, I believe there
must be what we might call an animals' heaven. And if there
is I am certain he is rejoicing in it.' We felt much happier
after our prayer together, reconciled about the rightness of
our decision to bestow upon Satan the dignity of a merciful
death. The day he died was the Wednesday of Holy Week
that year.

On the following Saturday morning I had to get up particularly early and went to make a cup of tea. While waiting
for the kettle to boil I felt a nudge on my shin which was
repeated several times. It was immediately familiar as the
action which Satan had performed every morning of his life
when I was engaged in this same chore. I would come down
each morning into the kitchen where he slept and, before
doing anything else, give him a saucer of milk and a bowl of
Puffed Wheat, which he adored. Then I would fill the kettle
for tea and wait for it to boil. As if to thank me he would
rub himself against my legs before asking to go out, which
he would do by standing near the window which opened
on to the garden.

It was so natural a sensation on this particular morning
that I said involuntarily, as if Satan were there: 'All right,

136

old thing. I'll let you out in just a minute.' Then I looked down for the first time and saw Satan. I bent down to stroke him, after which he moved away. It was only then that it occurred to me what a phenomenon I was witnessing. Satan had been put to sleep three days earlier and yet her he was, tangible and visible.

Doubtless I was in a state of partial trance at that exceptionally early hour, but the physical sensations of the cat's presence and the sight of him were as natural as could be. Only when I recollected his death did he disappear as if jumping through the closed window. Then something seemed to click inside my head. I could not help reflecting that the next day was Easter Day with its triumphant message of resurrection, and of the promise that all things would be made new.

Part 2
Reflections

1

THE SOUL

'Something which leaves the body when we die': so a class of teenagers answered my question as to what they understood by the soul. It was quite obvious to them that unless endowed with a life-force, the body is only a corpse. But they also realized that this life-force, or soul, is responsible for much more than a biological process.

They came to the conclusion that the soul operates on two levels:

1. The physiological, whereby the body is kept alive and has comprehension of the material world through the five sense perceptions.

2. The spiritual, whereby thoughts, emotions, and the creative power of the imagination carry us into a realm which is not purely materialistic but abstract. Through this level of the soul come art, philosophy, all manner of learning, and, of course, religion. Through it also comes the inspiration for all the noblest of man's activities; his love, courage, and self-sacrifice, and also, unfortunately, his worst characteristics as well.

The first level could be defined as the operation of the 'body-soul' and the second as that of the 'spirit-soul'. Yet, though for ease of definition we may speak of body-soul and spirit-soul, we must not think of there being two souls. There is but *one* soul expressing itself on these two levels.

However, there is what might be called a tug-of-war in human nature wherein the body-soul seeks to dominate or misdirect the highest aspiration of the spirit-soul. This downward pull is a universal fault in mankind which religion defines as 'sin'. Sin literally means 'missing the mark', that is a failure to reach the target of perfection which the spirit-soul conceives but, because of the contrary desires and weakness of the body-soul, cannot wholly realize. Man, then, is a 'fallen' creature. His potential perfection is ever marred by this universal grip of sin.

All this is pictorially represented in the creation story in the Bible's book of Genesis. The paradisal state of Adam and Eve, our first ancestors, is lost when they determine 'to hide from God' and choose to dominate their physical environment. This constituted a rebellion against their Creator, a usurpation of his supreme authority by challenging it in their material domain. Hence they came under the domination of matter as the body claimed pride of place over the spirit.

God's benevolent design was for his love towards Adam and Eve to be reciprocated so that perfect harmony might prevail between them and himself. Therefore he endowed them with free will by which, out of their own choice and not as mere puppets, they might love him and desire his will in all their ways. Their arrogance, therefore, meant an abuse of that free will. They chose to be their own gods, to have their own kingdom to themselves, a kingdom of this material world.

Two results were the consequence of this disobedience to the divine will.

1. Because they desired to rule matter they fell under its domination and became heirs to the properties of matter. Hence came decay and death, fatigue, disease, and suffering.

2. Because they had misused free will their will was weakened. Hence the powers of the spirit-soul were greatly curtailed, since the will is the high attribute of the soul.

So the full glory of man's nature was diminished. Nevertheless he retains vestiges of the originally perfect powers of the spirit-soul by virtue of the fact that though he is imperfect yet he is still made in the likeness of God. The Spirit of God dwells in him.

When, therefore, the spirit-soul is freed, or partially freed, from the domination of the body-soul, those vestigial powers can be exercised. These include the phenomena of telepathy, clairvoyance, precognition, prophecy, healing, divination, visions, as well as certain physical feats which could not be performed in the ordinary state. The reason for these phenomena lies in the nature of the properties of pure spirit. 'A pure spirit', as Abbot Weisinger reminds us, 'is immortal, not subject to suffering, can influence matter, has an understanding that knows all things to which it directs its attention with absolute clarity, and possesses a will which holds fast to all that is presented to it by its understanding.'

Within the framework of this definition we can perceive why rudimentary extra-sensory faculties are manifested when the domination of the body-soul is suspended. They are rudimentary and imperfect because of the diminution of the powers of the spirit by the grip of sin. Until all sin has been overcome there will not be pure spirit with the perfection of its powers. The hope of the Christian faith is, of course, that the power of sin has been 'dealt with by God acting in Jesus Christ'.

How can the spirit-soul be freed from the domination of the body-soul? The answer is through trance. In trance the awarenesses of the physical body are extinguished because the sense perceptions are suspended. The body-soul capitulates to the spirit-soul which can then exercise its powers without being subject to matter.

2

TRANCE

To free the spirit-soul from its domination by the body-soul the normal state of our being must be replaced by the special one of trance. Thus liberated, the spirit-soul can then perform as pure spirit and paranormal phenomena may occur.

The experiments of hypnosis furnish perhaps the best proofs of the powers of the spirit-soul. In hypnosis a state of trance is induced in the subject, who will then act out the controlling instructions of the hypnotist. The phenomena observed are extraordinary. Not only are the usual extra-sensory perceptions exhibited, but the power of the spirit-soul over its own physical body is demonstrated. The pulse and digestive system can be manipulated, as can the five senses and also the temperature of the body. The mind, because it is an attribute of the body-soul, can also be acted upon and so give rise to hallucinations and illusions as the hypnotist dictates. Even certain healings are possible. Sick people under hypnosis have been known to see inside their own bodies and diagnose foreign matter within them.

Feats of the body which could not be performed in the normal state also illustrate the powers of the spirit-soul over the physical limitations. To quote but two well-known examples: the subject can be supported at the head and the heels simply upon the backs of two chairs, remaining rigidly thus for as long as the hypnotist wishes, even when weights have been placed on the unsupported trunk; or the subject may hold a heavy weight effortlessly at arm's length until the hypnotist concludes the trance.

It is commonly thought that a hypnotized person can be made to do almost anything short of that which is contrary to his or her strong moral convictions. Yet even the latter can be broken down by intensive sessions of hypnotism, so that the subject is literally a puppet obeying every behest of the hypnotist.

Though it may be argued that hypnotism can be used to effect certain good in the medical field, it could be said that a moral principle has been violated inasmuch as the subject has lost some portion of freedom of the will which is the precious heritage of every human being. He or she is also susceptible henceforth to hypnotic influence. We may well then question the virtue of bending the will of another by this means, for even if the hypnotist is the most saintly character, he is still a fallible human being in whom the imperfection of sin abides. Moreover, even God does not impose his will by taking away the will of his creatures.

Those who have been present at a hypnosis will know the somewhat weird atmosphere which is generated and will intuitively recognize that there is something not quite healthy about it. It is, therefore, not to be encouraged as a way to attain out-of-the-body experiences. Such experiences hold fascination for many today. Hence the ardent desire so prevalent among the young for something which will release the spirit-soul from the encumbrance of the body-soul. To achieve this, and thus also escape from the gross and oppressive materialism of this modern age, many resort to drugs. Their use provides a short-cut to reducing the normal senses of the body and thus releases the spirit-soul so it may discover the delights of an out-of-the-body experience.

Such transports are very real to the drug-addicted, as those who have to deal with them soon learn. I have myself listened, quite fascinated at first, to the recital of visions and transcendental experiences which such people tell me they receive. However, one does not have to listen long before one perceives irrationality and incompleteness in all they disclose. The experiences are disjointed and bring a deterioration of the will. In the end there is but one consuming desire for drug addicts: to live only in the fantasy of their spiritual experience and have nothing to do with this world at all.

The fact is that only the guided or controlled trance such as the hypnotic one can provide rationality in the activity of the spirit-soul. Otherwise the experiences afforded by its freedom from the body-soul result in wild hallucinations and incoherence, which lead to an enfeebled mind or even madness. Accidental death is also a possibility as, for example, when the drugged person imagines he or she can fly or is oblivious to all dangers. Because the body-soul and the spirit-soul are meant to be true entities, the abuse of either will have a deleterious effect upon the other. So it is that the bodies of drug addicts become emaciated and sickly and there is premature death.

Trance can also be induced by loud and persistent drumming noises and flashing lights. After a time the senses are deadened and an out-of-the-body experience occurs. This is what takes place in the so-called psychedelic atmosphere when a group of people keep up a rhythmic and prolonged dance to the beat of pop music under special lighting effects. In this case there is a form of mass hypnosis engendered in which the spirit-souls of the participants are opened up to the mixture of the wills and desires of everyone present. In this muddle there can happen, at least for some of the more susceptible, an ecstatic delirium but one which exhausts and deadens rather than inspires and invigorates. A feeling of having entered another world can be experienced but it is a world of disordered fantasy, shadows, and irrelevance.

Self-hypnosis attained by staring at a candle flame, contemplating a flower, gazing at a crystal ball or other bright object, holding an article of special significance to the life of oneself or of someone else as in psychometry, or using such apparatus as the divining-rod, also produces the trance condition necessary to liberate the spirit-soul so that it can exercise its supernatural powers and acquire knowledge beyond that possible in the normal state.

Such self-hypnosis has the advantage that the spirit-soul faculties are harnessed to the rational world of matter because material objects are used to evoke the trance. These then control the ESP and make the latter relevant to this world. Unlike hypnosis by the mind of another person there is not here the danger of weakening the will, unless the practice is continued to the extent of becoming an obsession, when the person is likely to end up by living a twilight existence damaging to the health of the body.

Nevertheless this form of trance is circumscribed by its very means of induction. It furnishes not a really exalting spiritual experience but one which, on the whole, is trivial, though some usefulness may be afforded such as the discovery of lost objects or people or a knowledge of mineral and other deposits in the earth.

The remaining method of inducing trance is that of prayer, which uses abstract truths or religious concepts to hold the attention. As the concentration deepens, the mind opens up to further and further exploration of that on which it is meditating. The patient practice of prayer creates such profound absorption in the spiritual themes chosen that the sense perceptions drop away into the background of consciousness and the spirit-soul comes into its own and will then display the powers of pure spirit.

Prayer can be corporate or individual. Someone of greater spiritual insight can lead the meditation of a group, or the single soul can embark upon the path of prayer on his or her own. Both are fruitful and neither should be neglected if there is to be variety and depth to the spiritual life.

3

JESUS AND OURSELVES

We have seen how the biblical story of Adam and Eve symbolically portrays the fact of sin which affects all men in their human solidarity. Its origin was self-will and the rejection of the true mark which the Creator planned for his creatures.

The only way to redeem this situation and to restore to them their lost perfection was for the Creator to cause a new quality of human life to enter the world, a life lived in perfect accord with the divine will — a life in which the two levels of the soul's activity, body-soul and spirit-soul, were perfectly adjusted and reconciled. Because the life of Jesus Christ was totally obedient to the Creator's will, never succumbing to the temptation to sin, it can be said that in Jesus of Nazareth God was bringing human life into that accord with himself which is his design for it, reconciling it to himself.

Jesus was the unique son of God. He was true Man, man as he is meant to be in entire harmony with his Creator. The proof of this is his resurrection. The selfish desires of humanity could work their will upon Jesus, but after the crucifixion there was no more they could do to him. His spirit-soul was in full command and God declares the validity and ultimate victory of the spiritual realm of Christ through the resurrection whereby his unique Son reveals eternally the power and glory controlling the universe.

But, it will be said, in Jesus we have a special case. How can our own dilemma be resolved, this universal one of the domination in our lives of the power of sin? How, in other words, can this unique quality of Christ's life exist in us? The Christian answer is through faith. Faith is pre-eminently the faculty of the soul which acts on both levels, through body-soul and spirit-soul. By faith the believer is incorporated into the unique life which is in Christ. In spiritual terms, he lives now in Christ, and Christ in him.

It is the sheer simplicity of this that brings intellectual difficulty. Jesus sees this clearly. We have, he says, to become 'as little children', as uncomplicated and trusting as they in order to enter into this new triumphant life which he calls the Kingdom of God. There God rules, and it is by the exercise of that faculty of the soul called faith that we enter his kingdom. Although there is no need to discard entirely the working of the mind, we must accept that faith soars above the finite and the material and carries us into the realms of pure spirit.

Faith is the most powerful of all the faculties of the soul. Out of it can stem all good and, indeed, all evil. All mankind through all the centuries has lived by faith as a driving force. Where there is no faith, or faith only in that which is of this world, man's potential nobility declines, since his vision is limited. It bears the seed of decay and in time all hope is gone.

By faith in the Spirit of Christ, who is risen and eternally present, we become possessed of that same eternal quality of life which is his. As St Paul puts it, because he is risen we are risen also. By the mysterious working of faith we are partakers with him of the same endless and glorious life.

But this is an inheritance of the total soul of man. Signs of that higher life are manifested by the quality of thought and deed which Christ's life and teaching inspire. So faith in Christ is no passive thing. It is bound to include what is called the practical life, i.e. the exertions of the body-soul, which are inspired by the spirit-soul, to perform that which affects our neighbour's good and only his good.

However, we know well enough that the warfare continues between body-soul and spirit-soul in this life. Ardent in faith as he was, St Paul yet realized that the good he would do he did not perfectly accomplish, and the ill that he did not desire to do was often what in fact he practised. Such is the power of sin. Failure and imperfection, the result of the continuing domination of the body-soul, continue in our lives. Nevertheless by our attachment to Christ through the faculty of faith the battle with sin is assured of final victory.

By following the sinless Christ, conscientiously endeavouring to allow his attitudes and outlook to influence the conduct of our lives, we are letting his life raise up and govern our own. We are on the way to becoming 'new creatures', entering a new creation where the grip of sin in us is being extinguished. Life in this world is truly the 'vale of soul-making', but the fullness of life cannot be experienced while we are in the body of the flesh. Death comes and that body dissolves. Death is the perfect exodus to freedom, the way out of the old order to the fulfilment of our new creation wherein the spirit-soul is at last free from the domination of the body-soul.

But the soul is *one*. There is not body-soul *and* spirit-soul, for these are simply terms which define the levels of activity of one and the same soul. What, then, of the body-soul? Here the Christian faith supplies the same answer. The immortal spirit-soul does not continue after death in a kind of limbo, having only a shadowy existence. Our faith in Christ gives us a life like his. Because he lives we live also, and we are like him. So, through what must be a mystery this side of the grave, we are clothed with a new kind of body suited for the spiritual realm. Hence the soul which has known a body through which it can operate has not lost this aspect of its identity. The soul is made complete by the blessing of a spiritual body being given to it by God. To define-this body is impossible. It remains in this life a mystery beyond language and imagination because it needs the final experience of death before the transformation can come.

This spiritual body concept is in line with creation being an act of God's good pleasure. Out of love he was moved to make it and will not therefore eternally destroy it. Though sin, which is contrary to his will, has entered and pervaded his creatures, he will yet develop them to their perfection through a transformation. So he bestows upon those who love him a new kind of body which is free from the power of sin and therefore no more under the domination of matter and the temporal order, a spiritual body through which the eternal world shall be known and perfectly enjoyed.

4

DEMON-POSSESSION

In past ages belief in the power of demons undoubtedly re-
tarded man's progress. Science has largely removed that crip-
pling burden by finding rational and far more satisfactory
explanations for the ills of life than attributing them wholly
to the activity of evil entities. However, I do not think that
we can preclude altogether the possibility that some forms
of mental disease and paralysis may be due to what is called
demon-possession and that such, therefore, could be cured
by exorcism, whereby the expulsion of the offending demon
or demons from the afflicted person is effected.

One of the arguments against the idea of possession is that
the causes of those cases mentioned in the healing miracles
of Jesus can nowadays be better understood and mostly
cured by modern medicine. But it does not follow that all
disease is accounted for by the natural liability of our bodies.
There is, in fact, increasing proof for the view that in some
instances what sparks off an illness lies within the arena of
the various mental and spiritual conflicts plaguing our souls.
In other words, the personal factor cannot be ruled out in
explaining why some people fall victim to certain illnessess
and others do not. What are recognized today as psychosomatic afflictions support this view, and I believe that
among these an ever-widening field of disease will be included as this branch of medical knowledge advances.

It is surely not difficult to conceive that just as we can be
influenced for good or ill by the personality of another human being, so likewise we may be influenced by spirits which
have knowledge of us at our spirit-soul level. This suggests,
therefore, that we could receive the succour of angels and
also the malice of devils. If such spiritual entities exist, as I

believe they do, their effective action upon our lives would depend upon our willingness or otherwise to play host to them.

It appears likely that Jesus believed in demon-possession. He tells the story of a devil which had been exorcised from a man and then returned with seven other devils even worse than himself to torment the poor fellow still more. What we need to note most carefully is that Jesus never exercised a special form of exorcism or used any incantations to expel demons. He emphasized that evil spirits were removed solely by faith in the supreme power of God over them. So he claimed that divine power was acting through him when he cured men of demon-possession. For this reason he was more concerned with awakening in the possessed person, and also in the relatives and friends who were present, faith in God's complete sovereignty than with seeking belief in the power of exorcism. He declared that it was by the authority (i.e. power) of God that he delivered the sick from the assault of devils.

Only faith in God, then, casts out evil spirits, and the true exorcist acts upon this principle alone. Unfortunately many of those who believe in demon-possession are tempted to see cases of it everywhere, while the fact is that the actual discernment of demon-possession is an extremely difficult matter. Unexpected changes in a person's normal behaviour cannot always be attributed to the attack of demons. Quite often there is self-delusion on the part of those who may genuinely believe that they are possessed by devils. It can, of course, provide the unscrupulous with a convenient excuse to escape from personal responsibility for their actions.

My own experience with the sick suggests that in the beginning the laying-on of hands with prayer to bring spiritual healing is always the best course to pursue. This awakens the conscience of the sick person to the light of Jesus Christ and reassures his or her spirit-soul of the healing power, mercy, forgiveness, and love of God. Only when I have followed this path do I ever come to the conclusion as to whether or not there is possession by an evil spirit or spirits. In my own experience I have found such cases to be rare.

If convinced that there is an alien presence then I will conduct exorcism. My own prayer of preparation before giving the laying-on of hands will have strengthened my assurance of the presence of Christ, and in this conviction I address the demon, commanding it to leave the sick person and to enter that realm which God in his mercy has prepared for it and nevermore to return.

While it is true that I sometimes find exorcism causes a great tussle of will on my part I am certain, nevertheless, that a violent struggle in which my body is wracked by fierce tremors, as some exorcists generally manifest, is not necessarily the surest sign of successful contest with an evil entity. Rather I believe that the biblical advice should be accepted, and that in quietness and confidence shall be one's strength. Any personal agitation is surely a denial of this, for it cannot be underlined enough that exorcism is never effected through one's own spiritual power. What is required of the exorcist is a complete and steady faith in the sovereign authority of God over all spiritual beings.

5

SPIRITUAL HEALING

By the manner of his life Jesus Christ raised humanity to the level of divinity, into perfect union with the Creator. In him the defect of sin, universal in our human nature, was absent. Therefore he revealed upon this planet an entirely new order of creation, a sinless human being.

Sin causes us to be dominated by matter and thus subjugated to the properties of matter which include fatigue, pain, disease, change, decay, and death. If sin could be overcome we would have not only abundant, perfectly fulfilled, but also everlasting, life. Through that special faculty of our spirit-soul called faith we can enter a mystical union with Christ and so partake, here and now, of that new order of creation which he inaugurated.

Hence the would-be spiritual healer must first accept by faith what God has done in introducing through the life of Christ an order of being which transforms the old order. The old is under the dominion of matter; the new controls matter and transcends it. By meditation upon the life and teaching of Jesus the healer enters a condition of trance. His sense perceptions slip away, thus releasing his spirit-soul which will then act as pure spirit. He may now manifest extrasensory perceptions, including the certain knowledge of mystical union with the Spirit of Christ.

Before he engages upon the trance state the healer, out of compassion, wills that the spirit-soul of the sick person be also drawn into that union. Thus he and the patient are united in Christ and together become sharers of the new creation begun by him. So the physical comes under the dominion of spirit. The spirit-soul of the sick person now controls his body-soul and acts upon it to bring the harmony and healing which are the properties of that new creation.

My own method of transmitting spiritual healing is first to seek quietness within myself in order to enable me to concentrate wholly upon the purpose ahead. Then I direct not only the patient's thoughts but my own as well upon the healing power and love of God, using relevant scriptural texts and incidents in the life of Jesus to give this insight. I find the Gospel according to St John especially helpful; being so rich in imagery it provides much to feed the imagination.

After thus meditating for a while, the consciousness of my surroundings gradually ceases and trance begins. There follows the sense that my body is, as it were, simply a shell or garment, and I appear to be floating free of it in an atmosphere of peculiar light and warmth which is also pulsing with a strange energy. The mental pictures stimulated by St John's Gospel begin to be controlled and expanded as though by a power beyond myself, and I know that I am being related to the wondrous presence of Christ and that realm in which he rules absolutely.

I desire to draw the sick person also into that presence, and so together we receive the healing that his new creation bestows. It is only then that I give the laying-on of my hands. It is very important, I believe, to use in my meditations not simply the words, be they of prayers or texts, but to embrace them always, as I utter them, in clear mental pictures, including my desire to bring the sick person into Christ's presence. Thus word language is transcended by picture language, which communicates its message from my spirit-soul to the spirit-soul of the person whom I wish to help in a way which is particularly necessary in those cases where the sick person is incapable of hearing because of deafness or unconsciousness, or perhaps does not understand English. If people are very ill I may not always speak to them or pray with them but instead bid my spirit-soul to make direct contact with their spirit-souls as I kneel at their side.

It cannot be over-emphasized that this healing is essentially spiritual. That is, it concerns the making whole of the spirit-soul by bringing to it comfort, inspiration, confidence, hope, and trust in God's eternal and constant love towards it. Whether, therefore, complete physical restoration ensues is not the primary purpose of spiritual healing. All must be understood to be in the hand of God who is all-wise and all-good. It is solely through faith in him that our healing comes. By that faith we are made whole. Sickness is never the will of God for his human creatures, but it can be the means through which we can come to know him very deeply and in a special way, and thus bring to us the most precious inward joy and peace.

Physical recovery may, and often does, follow because the healing of the spirit-soul must affect the body-soul. Spiritual healing integrates our personality. It harmonizes our body-soul and our spirit-soul. Moreover, the soul which is in Christ through such spiritual healing does not have to be anxious about the sickness of the body since it knows when the time comes there will be given to it by God a new kind of body, a spiritual one. Through this new body the soul will experience the fullness of life in a purely spiritual realm where the physical world's order of suffering, decay, and death is transcended.